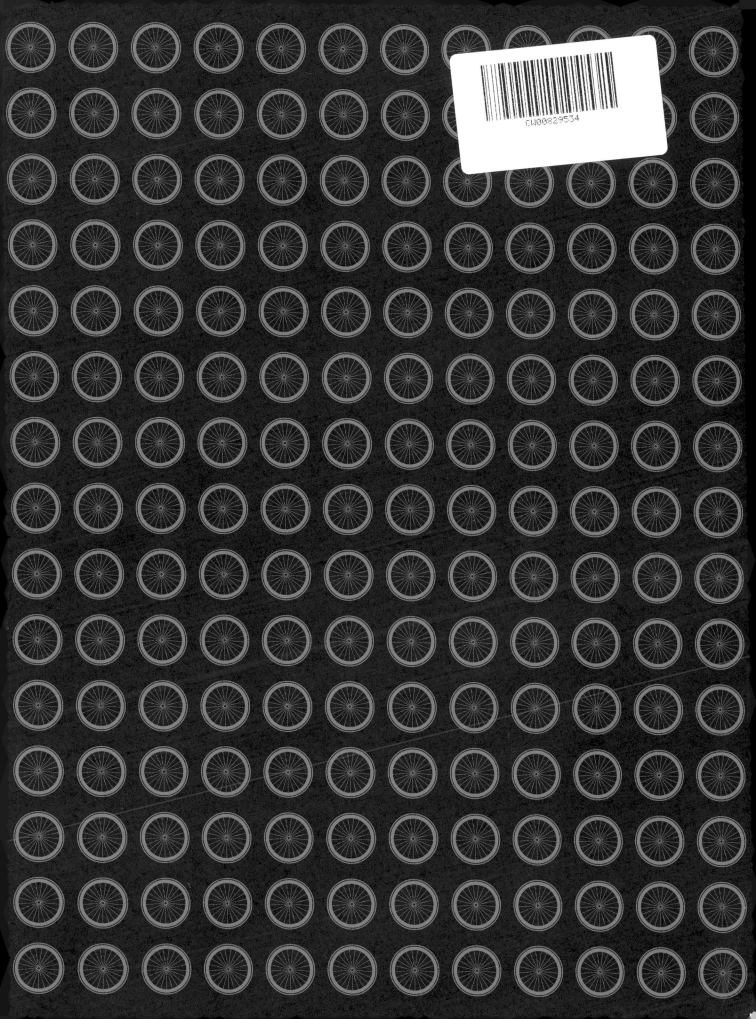

The New Grand Tour Cookbook
Copyright © Helmin & Sorgenfri
and Musette Publishing, 2023

Photo: Hannah Grant
Rider pictures: Scanpix
Picture collage: BrakeThrough Media
Editorial staff: Hannah Grant og Jesper Helmin

ISBN: 978-87-94190-20-6
1. edition, 1. circulation
Printed in EU

Other books by Hannah Grant:
The Cake Cookbook
Eat Race Win
The Grand Tour Cookbook

More info:
hannahgrant.com
@dailystews

www.helminsorgenfri.dk

THE NEW Grand TOUR COOKBOOK

HANNAH GRANT

TABLE OF CONTENT

About
HANNAH
GRANT

In 2013, my first cookbook – The Grand Tour Cookbook – was published. In many ways, The Grand Tour Cookbook changed the sport of cycling's approach to food and nutrition by thinking about food as a whole for cyclists. Food was no longer just fuel – it was recovery, comfort, a morale booster, a band-aid after a bad day, or the celebration after a win. Suddenly, food was a holistic element in and around performance and recovery in ways not thought of before.

The recipes were based on functional foods and whole, pure ingredients, without excessive amounts of overprocessed ingredients. It was moving; it was groundbreaking; and it was perhaps also at times a little more extreme than the way people worked – even so today, more than a decade later. I'll get into that later, but first, here's my story.

I was born in Aarhus but grew up in Copenhagen. I have a Danish mother and a Scottish father who both worked in the magical world of the theater, so it was a creative and liberal home, with no expectations of a university education or a nine-to-five office job. I have always enjoyed cooking and probably ate better food compared to other kids in my neighborhood in the 1980s and 1990s.

My father was a skilled cook and experimented quite a lot in the kitchen. My grandmother was one of Scotland's first female head chefs, and her name was also Hannah Grant, so maybe it was in the cards that cooking would be my way of living. If so, thank you so much, Grandma.

However, my road to the kitchen was not as straight and flat as an early Tour de France stage. I had some detours. After primary school, I started high school somewhat reluctantly, as my mother refused to let me go to Culinary school because I was too young, and my mom believed that everyone in the industry was full blown alcholics, so I'd better stay clear of that mess.

I did well in high school, at least socially. But I had a problem, one that I probably shared with many others who choose the path of a chef – high school did not interest me at all. I was far too restless and unable to focus. I had all this energy. Something had to happen – I had to do something creative. After two years and a few months, I dropped out of high school at 18 – old enough to plot my own course. I immediately began working full time at my weekend job in the perfume department at the Magasin du Nord shopping mall while trying to figure out what to do next. You might be thinking, "Well, then you started culinary school." Nope! I joined the Navy.

My friend had signed up and said, "It's so cool; you have to do it!" I thought, "Okay, it's nine months, and I actually need a kick in the ass to move on. Maybe the Navy will toughen me up and do some good." So, I signed up and began with basic training at Camp Auderød in October 2002, followed by Combat Academy in Frederikshavn. Ready to set sail, we did a double tour with HDMS Hvidbjørnen patrolling the waters around Greenland, the Faroe Islands, and Iceland.

One day, I was standing in the galley talking to my friend Carl, the ship's chef. He asked me to season a bathtub sized pot of bechamel sauce, and whilst I was paddling around in the sauce, it hit me – I'M GONNA BE A CHEF! A true epiphany, so when I got home, I signed up for culinary school. My time in the Navy certainly prepared me to handle the rough and tough and hierarchy of a professional kitchen and, later, of a pro-cycling team.

The chef world was very male-dominated, and you had to stick up for yourself and work and talk hard. In 2007, I got my chef's diploma and was determined to go out into and experience the world and improve my skills. In the following years, I had exciting jobs and experiences working at Michelin star restaurants such as The Fat Duck and Noma. I was also part of a kiteboarding expedition that sailed around some of the most desolate places in the world, from the Galapagos Islands and French Polynesia to the Northern Cook Islands and the Kingdom of Tonga.

My time as a chef was full of different experiences and tastes, but it was not to be the last time that my job would take me on an exciting trip.

A NEW CYCLING WORLD DAWNS

In autumn 2010, I was offered the job as chef for the then Danish pro-cycling team owned by Bjarne Riis. The team had decided they needed a new chef, with a Michelin star background, who could radically change the team's diet. I was chosen from three other highly qualified chefs.

I was the first female chef in cycling and quickly got a lot of attention from interested media worldwide - a brilliant PR move (I can't say if that was the idea behind it, but it worked anyway).

The plan was ambitious – the team was to develop a completely new nutritional strategy, where variety, taste, and pure ingredients were to be part of the daily life of the team's riders. I clearly remember the conversation I had with the physical therapist who carried out the first interviews: "Well, you see, it's three or four days of travel,

and then you have a week or two off before going back on the road." It sounded extremely cool, as a chef, to be able to travel around Europe and cook for top athletes, where training and diet was the alpha and omega.

I instantly accepted the job, which turned out to be a little more demanding than I had first thought. I had about 140 travel days a year with the team, which included two training camps, a lot of smaller stage races, and all three Grand Tours each year. As the only employee on the team, I therefore took part in all the Grand Tours; Giro d'Italia, Tour de France, and Vuelta España every year – in addition to all the other races.

A DIFFICULT BEGINNING

My start with the team was rough – to say the least. The older and more seasoned riders were used to pasta and ketchup, and here I was with all my fancy ideas, making all the food from scratch, with lots of delicious dishes and many variations – but no white pasta. It wasn't a hit at first, let me tell you that!

The first year was an uphill struggle, and many of the riders saw me as the devil in the kitchen armed with quinoa, brown rice, fish, gluten-free bread, and vegetables – all on order from the boss. The riders were longing for the crappy, but well know hotel buffet with soggy fries and white pasta.

I remember it clearly; I was so surprised that some of the world's best athletes were completely indifferent to what the team had planned for their diet and nutrition, and it dawned on me that my new job would not be a walk in the park. On the contrary, it was an interesting challenge – to determine the optimal nutrition, as desired by the team, and actually get the riders to eat it. That was the number one challenge on my list. The second was to prepare food that the riders liked, while the third was to get them to request their new favorite dishes. Let me just say that it didn't happen overnight.

THE SUCCESSFUL 2:1 RATIO AND A COOKBOOK LATER

After the first season with the team, I gradually cracked the code to get the riders to like my food. I used the 2:1 ratio if I wanted them to taste something new. It was simple, but it worked: two parts familiar ingredients that were high on the list of things they liked and one part "new" (or less loved) ingredients.

With the 2:1 ratio, the riders didn't generally bother to sit and sort through their food, and so the less loved ingredients got eaten – often with the revelation that they actually liked it!
In this way, the list of ingredients and flavors the riders liked grew, and it became more fun to cook for them.

In 2013, The Grand Tour Cookbook was published, based on my many hours of work with the cycling team. There was widespread interest in the book, and it open the door for me as a chef on TV. The Grand Tour Cookbook quickly became very popular and, in the following years, was published in five languages: Danish, English, German, French, and Czech.

AFTER THE CYCLING TEAM

After five years working full time with the cycling team, it was time for a new adventure. In 2016, I started working as a recipe and product developer for one of Denmark's largest meal box companies and as a food consultant for several larger cycling teams.

In 2016, I was back in Denmark for the month of July, for the first time in half a decade, traveling around with "TV2 on Tour" and cooking from local ingredients every day. My recipe development work continued, all the while working on a new book – Eat Race Win – when I was approached with a crazy offer. The English version of The Grand Tour Cookbook had miraculously ended up in the hands of an American producer who wanted to produce a mini documentary

series about me and my work. It was the start of a wild project and a six-episode, Emmy-winning TV series on Amazon Prime, which we filmed during the Tour de France in 2017 and which premiered in 2018 (pssst... you can still watch it). More was to follow – in January 2018, I was hired to do the cooking for a 100-man-strong TV team covering the Dakar Rally, which ran through Peru, Bolivia, and Argentina.

Since then, I worked on product development related to hydration and sleep and continued with recipe development.

In 2022, The Cake Cookbook was released – a book of cakes perfect for training. You should definitely check it out. But right now, you're sitting with this yellow book in your hands - thank you so much for that!

I hope you will join me on the future path of exciting performance recipes. I promise it will not be boring.

HANNAH GRANT

FOLLOW ME HERE:
Instagram: @dailystews
Facebook: Hannah Grant /
             hannahgrantcooking
Youtube: @HannahGrant
Web: hannahgrant.com

Hannahs
PALMARES

16 Grand Tours

6 x Tour de France

5 x Giro d'Italia

5 x Vuelta a España

4 Grand Tour wins

1 TDF mountain jersey

1 TDF points jersey

780 days of cycling

Approx. 1 ton of pasta

11.040+ eggs

2000+ chickens

20 million+ calories − in Grand Tours only

450+ different hotels

3000+ cups of coffee

7 National champions

1 World champion

52 stage wins

INTRODUCTION to
THE NEW GRAND TOUR COOKBOOK

This book is for those who love the Tour de France... and for those who love cycling. Whether you are a dedicated Tour de France fan or active on the road – this book is for you.

Since working with pro-riders, much more specific ways of working with diet have been developed, but the essence is still the same – As a danish proverb says: Without food and drink, the hero cannot perform. The fact is that good, varied and sufficient food is needed to complete a Tour de France, and it is clearly a bonus if it is also delicius (and easy to make at home).

The New Grand Tour Cookbook takes you through an entire Tour de France, with easy and delicious recipes for the whole family. Everyone can benefit from the beginner to the passionate and seasoned rider - and even those who just watch the Tour de France can get a taste of the Tour.

The recipes are based on my Tour food philosophy, which focuses on quality ingredients, delicious combinations, and easy recipes that anyone can make. Even the riders!

The recipes are easy to adapt, so they can fit into your specific diet – whether you live without dairy products, avoid gluten, or would like to adjust the macronutrients to suit your plan.

The keyword in the book is balance, so there are plenty of opportunities to find the dishes you like and that work for you.

The recipes are based on the philosophy behind The original Grand Tour Cookbook, which em- phasizes that cooking should be fun, easy, and manageable. We are not all the same, so work from the guidelines you find in this book and get inspiration from the riders to tailor a diet that is perfect for you.

In the book, you will not find any calorie calculations for the dishes. The reason for this is that I generally do not recommend counting calories (unless you are at an elite level or in the process of controlled weight loss). If you need to know the calories or have a macro breakdown of a recipe, find this online by scanning the QR code on the nutrition page.

In the book, you will find interviews with active and former riders and gain an insight into how they eat and what works for them. You will also read stories about the diet and training of previous generations of riders and gain an understanding of how the focus on diet has changed over the decades. It is quite a story – not only about food but also culture.

All the recipes are healthy and nutritious for the whole family, and if you are an avid cyclist, there are great recipes to fuel even the longest of rides.

FOREWORD
by BJARNE RIIS

I remember my first year as a professional rider. My sports director was a Belgian, Guillaume Driessens, a true legend. He was the sports director for Eddy Merckx who believed we should eat steaks because Merckx had eaten a lot of steaks in his time. During the Tour of Belgium, there was a day with two stages. We had steaks for breakfast, steaks between the two stages, and in the evening, of course, we had a steak. Steak three times in one day, all of them as tough as the sole of a shoe.

This was certainly not optimal for digestion or performance, but it is a good story. Since then, nutrition and gaining knowledge about it have become very important to me. As an athlete, I think it is very important to be aware of what is needed for good nutrition. For example, if you are struggling with the Alpe d'Huez, and your body has one excess kilogram, you will lose 45 seconds. And there were five climbs before the finish line at the top of the Alpe d'Huez. The seconds add up, and you lose valuable time.

That is why I gave priority to my own cycling team's nutrition. It's all about marginal gains to optimize the body's performance, get the best out of the riders, and at the same time, keep them motivated. I used to be a rider, so I understand what it's like to sit at shitty o'clock every morning and eat cooked pasta. It's not the most uplifting start to the day. It has always been difficult to get athletes to eat optimally with the right ingredients and nutrients. They have often complained that the food was boring and uninspiring. So, it was about creating an attractive diet. Add some color, make it look good and taste delicious. Hannah Grant certainly pushed some boundaries when she was on board.

How many ways can you cook chicken? It's a good protein that's easy to find, but the riders get bored just looking at it. It was necessary to create different chicken dishes that tasted distinct from day to day. I have always had a creative mind and looked for ways to improve things the best possible ways. My cycling team was among the best in the world, but where could we improve? On the diet, for sure. I believe it was a natural progression for us to advance our way of thinking about food and nutrition. And we did that.

It is important to know your own body. What works for me and what doesn't? Top athletes, especially riders, often feel they must starve themselves. But you don't have to be afraid to eat, you just have to learn to eat the right things at the right time, and then find out what ingredients are right for your body. You don't have to be afraid of fat, as long as it's the right kind. You don't have to be fanatical; you just have to be aware of what you are doing.

Enjoy the book, fuel well and ride fast!

BJARNE RIIS

THE NEW *Grand* TOUR COOKBOOK

- guidelines

Make your food from scratch.

Use quality products – preferably organic.

Follow the seasons.

Remember healthy fats.

Avoid processed foods.

Do not use artificial sweeteners.

Eat varied and colorful food.

Familiarize yourself with basic nutrition.

Get to know your body –
we are not all built the same.

BASIC KNOWLEDGE *of* NUTRITION

To perform optimally, you need to take good care of your body and eat a healthy, varied diet – and at the right times.

There is no shortcut or crash diet that can give you a strong and healthy body – it takes time and must be built up and maintained; fortunately, the way forward is delicious and tasty and can be easily incorporated into your everyday life at a pace that suits you.

To get the most out of your training, you must understand what, how, and when to eat so that you can perform at your best. What you eat and when you eat matter. The choice of your meals and the timing of them can have a decisive effect on your performance and recovery, which is essential for building muscle and having enough energy to get back on the bike day after day, ready to conquer the roads.

The right combination of carbohydrates, protein, and fat, with proper training, is the key to optimal performance.

If you think the following is a little text-heavy, you can always start by reading the introductions and summaries for each macronutrient and come back and read more when you're ready.

CARBO-HYDRATES

You know them, and you eat them every day. Carbohydrates come in many shapes and forms – fruit, vegetables, bread, pasta, rice, potatoes, sugar, soda, and cakes – and there is definitely room for all forms in a well-balanced diet.

Carbohydrates consist of sugar molecules that your body breaks down into fuel/energy so that you can move, think, and function optimally, and the more active you are, the more fuel you need. It's that simple. Carbohydrate can be divided into two categories: simple and complex carbohydrates.

Simple carbohydrates, in their simplest form, contain either one or two sugar molecules, e.g., ordinary sugar, cane sugar, fruit sugar, glucose, milk sugar, honey, and maple syrup. This is the nutrient source that the body can absorb the fastest.

Complex carbohydrates consist of many linked sugar molecules and thus take longer for the body to break down before absorbing. Complex carbohydrates include foods such as vegetables, potatoes, rice, pasta, oatmeal, quinoa, and other types of grains and starches. In general, complex carbohydrates are considered a healthier choice because they provide sustained energy and are a good source of fiber, vitamins, and minerals.

However, it is not that simple. There is a time and place for everything, and when it comes to very active people and athletes, the body must be able to access sources of energy quickly and efficiently, which makes simple carbohydrates the most optimal choice. However, it is important to understand that one needs to eat a varied diet rich in dietary fiber to take good care of your digestion.

Simple carbohydrates are a quick source of energy, which is essential during exercise. However, think about the quantity and timing any intake of simple carbohydrates outside of training, as the calorie content is often high and the nutrient content low, while also affecting blood sugar levels.

Blood sugar, also called glucose, is the main source of energy for the body. When we eat, the carbohydrates in our food are broken down into glucose, which enters the blood.

The pancreas, located just behind the stomach, produces the hormone insulin, which helps move glucose from the blood into the body's cells, transformed into energy. How much energy you need depends on how active you are, so if you have a very sedentary job and drive back and forth, you need much less energy than if you cycle 100 km a day and have a demanding physical job. You can read more about energy intake when riding later in this book.

So, what if you eat a giant bowl of sweets whilst slouching on the couch?

Blood sugar levels rise, as there is a sudden increase in the amount of glucose in the blood. Therefore, to stabilize blood sugar levels, the pancreas produces more insulin to move the excess glucose from the blood into the muscle cells, which can cause blood sugar levels to drop rapidly. A rapid drop in blood sugar can lead to fatigue, irritation, and hunger.

The excess glucose that the body does not use immediately is stored in the liver and muscles as glycogen. The muscles can store around 4 g

of glycogen per 100 g of muscle and a further approximately 100–120 g of glycogen in the liver; beyond that, everything else is converted into fat and stored in the body's adipose tissue.

A diet low in fiber, consisting of mainly simple carbohydrates, combined with a sedentary lifestyle, can lead to chronically high blood sugar levels and an increased risk of developing diabetes – so remember the vegetables on the dining table.

SUMMARY: Carbohydrate is a macronutrient with four calories per gram. We cannot live without carbohydrates (thankfully), but to get the most out of them, we can do ourselves a huge favor and choose when we eat which type of carbohydrate.

So, if you are sitting on your sofa right now, reading this, and thinking, "My pants are getting a little tighter," then you may need to keep an eye on when you eat which type of carbohydrate – a very small change in your daily diet can lead to big results – and looser pants.

FAT

As a rider, your body and brain are under extreme amounts of pressure every day, and in order for you to be the best version of yourself, it is important to keep the engine and the control tower, i.e., your body and brain, healthy and on track.

Fat is an essential part of a well-balanced diet, and it plays an extremely important role in how well our brain, nervous system, and body work. It has several functions in the body – helping with the absorption of fat-soluble vitamins such as A, D, E, and K; storing energy; insulating our body from the cold; and protecting our organs and nerve pathways – and then there is our control tower, our brain, which is made of 60% fat. When the brain is functioning optimally, our reaction time, ability to think clearly and quickly, and spatial awareness are at their peak. As a rider, this is a top priority if you want to be the best. Or one of them.

To tailor your diet to optimize your physical and cognitive performance, you need to understand the different types of fat, which are classified according to their chemical structure; don't worry – you don't have to be a chemist to figure this out.

TYPES OF FAT
Unsaturated fatty acids can be divided into two groups: monounsaturated and polyunsaturated fatty acids. Unsaturated fatty acids are usually liquid at room temperature and are found in fatty fish and plant-based foods such as nuts, seeds, and vegetable oils. Monounsaturated fatty acids are found in high-fat fruits such as avocados and olives, but also in nuts such as pistachios, almonds, walnuts, and cashews.

Monounsaturated fatty acids can help lower bad cholesterol (LDL) and raise good cholesterol (HDL) and can help prevent weight gain.

POLYUNSATURATED FATTY ACIDS
Polyunsaturated fatty acids contain the essential fatty acids Omega 3 (found in, e.g., fatty fish and shellfish such as anchovies, herring, mackerel, salmon, sardines, and oysters and in flaxseeds, chia seeds, and walnuts) and Omega 6 (found in, e.g., walnuts, grape seed oil, pine nuts, and sunflower seeds).

We must add Omega 3 and Omega 6 to the diet as our body cannot produce them itself. Unsaturated fats containing Omega 3 and Omega 6 fatty acids are important for brain function because they help support the structure of the brain and the function of brain cells. Unsaturated fats are an important component of the brain cell membrane, which acts as a barrier controlling what enters and exits the cell. The membrane is composed of a double layer of fat, and unsaturated fats help to make it more flexible so that nutrients can enter the cells and waste products can leave them. They also play a role in the production of certain brain chemicals called neurotransmitters, which help send signals between nerve cells so that you can move, breathe, think, and, yes, ride your bike.

CAN FISH OILS BOOST YOUR PERFORMANCE AND STRENGTHEN YOUR BRAIN?
Countless experiments and studies have been carried out on the effect of Omega 3 fatty acids, which indicate that it can have a positive effect on sports performance both for elite athletes and, to a greater extent, for amateurs.

A test conducted on female elite soccer players showed that reaction time and decision-making were significantly improved in players who consumed 3.5 g of fish oil with Omega 3 fatty acids daily compared to players who consumed 3.5 g of olive oil daily over a period of four weeks. Scientific articles indicate that Omega 3 fatty acids DHA and EPA play a major role in improved endurance, motor skills, and recovery for athletes and, to an even greater extent, amateurs[1].

There is also good news for the over 40s. Studies[2] have shown that a higher intake of Omega 3 fatty acids is associated with an improved ability to understand and solve complex problems using logical thinking, in addition to a larger hippocampus volume, which is the part of the brain involved in learning and memory processes. In short, this suggests that a daily intake of fish oils helps keep the brain and memory sharp throughout life.

Saturated fatty acids are typically solid at room temperature and are often found in animal products such as meat, butter, and cheese. Saturated fat is a compact source of energy, and our bodies store excess energy from carbohydrate as saturated fat in our adipose tissue for later use.

It is recommended that you keep your intake of saturated fat to a maximum of 10% of your daily energy intake to avoid a negative impact on your health. However, there are several new studies[3] indicating that we may have the wrong image of saturated fats and that it does not matter which source they come from or what the overall dietary intake looks like. However, when we talk about diet for a rider, saturated fatty acids are not high on the list of priorities.

Trans fat is a type of unsaturated fat that has been chemically altered to make it solid, margarine is a well-known example. Trans fats are often found in factory-processed foods such as chips, cookies, crackers, and deep-fried foods. The trans fatty acid process was invented in 1901 by a German chemist who discovered that he could stabilize vegetable oils through a chemical

process, the result being a cheaply produced alternative to butter, which the food industry quickly adopted.

To this day, the food industry still uses trans fatty acids in the production of processed foods, but more and more countries have banned them. However, Denmark limits the value to 2%, whereas in the United Kingdom, it is only a recommendation for food producers to avoid trans fatty acids. There are absolutely no health reasons to consume trans fatty acids, either for athletes or ordinary people, as they increase bad cholesterol levels, lower good ones, and significantly increase the risk of heart disease.

SUMMARY: Fat is a macronutrient with nine calories per gram. It is one of the most important sources for optimal performance both on and off the bike, but it matters what type of fat you eat. A daily intake of unsaturated fatty acids can help to influence your performance on the bike for the better, keep the brain sharp long into life, and help lower cholesterol levels and reduce the risk of cardiovascular disease. The right choice of fat is your friend and remember – Eat your fatty fish, your brain and body will thank you.

PROTEIN

As a rider, it is important to have strong muscles. The stronger your muscles are, the more watts you produce. Watt is a term for how much power you, as a rider, can transfer to the pedals – the more watts, the faster you go.

Every time you exercise, parts of your muscle fibers are broken, after which they rebuild to become stronger and more durable. For the muscles to repair themselves, amino acids must be added to your diet in the form of protein. For a cyclist, it is especially important to add protein right after training to recover optimally, build up the muscles, and thereby avoid excessively sore legs and fatigue the following day. Proteins are found in many foods, including meat, fish, poultry, beans, legumes, nuts, and eggs.

WHAT ARE AMINO ACIDS?

Amino acids are the building blocks from which proteins are forged. There are 20 different amino acids, of which nine are essential, which means that we cannot form them ourselves in the body but instead must be supplied via our diet.

Amino acids can vary in their structure and function, which makes it possible for proteins to have many different properties and functions in the body. For example, some amino acids are involved in forming hormones and enzymes, while others are important for building and repairing tissues (read muscles). It is important to cover your daily protein needs in your diet, to get enough amino acids (building blocks), for the body to maintain and build cells and tissues and keep all functions and processes going – so that you can ultimately become faster and stronger on the bike.

ANIMAL OR PLANT-BASED PROTEINS

Protein is protein, whether it comes from animals or plants. The difference between plant and animal protein is in their amino acid profile and bioavailability. We call them either complete or incomplete protein sources.

Protein from animal sources such as as egg, poultry, fish, and meat are complete proteins, as they are a good source of all the essential amino acids the body needs. Complete proteins cover all your amino acid needs and are easy for the body to absorb and use. Animal protein is also a good source of other nutrients, such as iron, zinc, and B vitamins.

Plant-based proteins, such as beans, legumes, nuts, seeds, and vegetables, are incomplete proteins. They can be lower in one or more essential amino acids and therefore do not contain all the essential amino acids in a single source (such as animal protein). It can also be more difficult for the body to absorb and use the amino acids.

Since the protein content per 100 g of raw material is lower in plant-based proteins, the amount of food you must consume to cover your protein and amino acid needs can therefore be quite large, and if you race a stage race or train heavy several days in a row, it can be a challenge to consume such large amounts of food.

Let's compare the protein content of cooked chicken breast and boiled chickpeas: Chicken contains approximately 20 g of protein per 100 g, and chickpeas contain approximately 7–8 g of protein per 100 g. This means that you have to eat almost three times as much boiled chickpeas by weight compared to chicken breast to get the same amount of protein; in other words, it is not impossible to be on a 100% plant-based diet as a cyclist, but it is demanding and difficult.

If you want to go 100% plant-based, you must familiarize yourself with how and from which protein sources to get your full amino acid needs covered. It is essential to vary your diet and combine different plant-based proteins to get sufficient amounts of all the essential amino acids to recover properly. However, if you eat dairy products, eggs, or fish, you are pretty well covered.

PROTEIN PROVIDES SATIETY

If you get hungry during the day even though you have eaten breakfast and lunch, you may need to look at your protein intake. Protein keeps you full for longer as it takes longer to digest than carbohydrates or fat. Protein can therefore help to reduce the urge to eat intermediate meals or snacks during the day. Protein also helps regulate blood sugar levels and increases the release of the hormone leptin, which regulates feelings of satiety.

And now you may be thinking: "Allright... I'll just grab a protein bar, and then the problem is solved." However, you have to be aware that the majority of all protein bars that proclaim to have a high protein content also typically have a high carbohydrate content in the form of sugar, which does not do much good other than contributing to an increased and most likely unnecessary energy intake (unless you are on the bike, in which case the protein does not makes much sense). Therefore, do yourself a favor and increase the amount of protein in your larger meals.

HOW MUCH PROTEIN SHOULD I HAVE?

The amount of protein you should consume depends on how active you are; your age; the intensity of your training, exercise, and running program; and your gender. When you reach the age of 40, your muscle mass starts to disappear faster if you don't keep it up, and therefore your protein intake must be adjusted accordingly.

Here is a general recommendation for daily intake of protein by activity level.[4].

Men

0.83 g per kg of body weight: sedentary or only light physical activity daily.
1.2–1.4 g per kg of body weight: hobby athletes.
1.4–1.6 g per kg of body weight: serious amateur athletes.
1.4–2.0 g per kg of body weight: elite athletes.

Women

Overall, active women should be 0.4 g higher than men, between *1.7–2.4 g per kg of body weight*.
Pre-menopause: *1.8–2.2 g per kg of body weight*.
Women in menopause (menopause): *2–2.4 g per kg of body weight*[10]

Women generally need more protein than men to activate protein buildup. Specifically[5], the content of the amino acid leucine must be higher, especially for women over 60. Studies show that protein intake must be evenly distributed between all meals and be between 25–30 g per meal[6] to maintain muscle mass.

If you are a female athlete and would like to optimize your performance, I recommend that you check out my reading list.

SUMMARY: Protein is a macronutrient containing four calories per gram. You can't perform or ride without protein; in fact, you can't function on a daily basis without protein, at least not in the long run. Protein is the building block that repairs and rebuilds your muscles and helps make you stronger and more durable between each workout. Therefore, it is important that you remember to eat protein at every meal – and especially after exercising.

ALCOHOL

Whether you love wine, beer, or liquor, there is unfortunately nothing performance enhancing to say about alcohol other than that you can celebrate a victory with a glass.

If you want to get in better shape and loose a few kilos, then alcohol is the first place to start. Yes, this sounds like a party killer, but there is no getting around the fact that alcohol is in no way necessary for the body and is just empty calories. I am not saying that you must never touch a drop again, but I am telling you that if you want to be serious about your sport, then your alcohol intake must be at an absolute minimum.

Alcohol has a dehydrating effect and a relatively high calorie content of seven calories per gram, which the body can only convert into fat. Your body prioritizes alcohol combustion before anything else, as it is a solvent and toxin that can affect the brain and cells in the body if it is not removed quickly.

So remember, do enjoy a glass every now and then, however just give it some thought wether or not it makes sense in terms fo your caloric intake. Remember to hydrate with a proper electrolyte product before during and after you consume alcohol, this way your hydration levels will be back on track faster.

And with those words; Cheers to that.

VITAMINS & MINERALS

If you eat a varied diet, you will most likely meet your daily vitamin and mineral needs.

There are, of course, some exceptions. If you do not eat meat, fish, eggs, or dairy products at all, it may be beneficial to check whether you are getting enough iron, as this is essential for the production of red blood cells. The red blood cells set the capacity for how much oxygen you can transport to your muscles, and if you have a reduced supply of oxygen to your muscles, you will be tired and have no energy to get on the bike.

The body can produce vitamin D itself when the skin is exposed to direct sunlight. However, it can be difficult to get enough vitamin D in the winter if you live in the northern hemisphere, and therefore it may be a good idea to check out if you need a supplement of vitamin D, which is essential for optimal calcium absorption and bone formation – and it is important for a rider to have strong bones to perform optimally.

Remember, always consult a health professional if you're in a doubt.

NO QUICK-FIX DIETS

BODY WEIGHT AND BODY COMPOSITION

The number on the bathroom scale can be a good indicator of the your bodys condition, however, do not let the scale dictate your life.

As a rider, every gram of weight on the body counts – it's all about having the best power to weight ratio. When the number on the bathroom scale is not what you hoped for, it can quickly change your mood. As an elite cyclist, it is important to be "lean," i.e., have a low fat percentage and a large muscle mass. However, for many people, it's a delicate balance to keep track of your weight without being overly focused on every single calorie, skipping meals or starving yourself to cut calories in the hope of quick weight loss.

However, your weight does not provide the full picture, as this relates to the total weight of your entire body, which consists of muscles, fat, bones, and fluid, and the proportion between these are not the same. Your weight can look like it is standing still or increasing, even if you increase muscle mass at the same time as decreasing your fat percentage. Therefore, if you struggle with your weight or just want to know what your body composition is, it might be a good idea to get it measured by an expert.

Some riders use a DEXA scan, which is the most accurate body scan available, but it is difficult and expensive to have such a measurement taken. There are other options, such as an InBody measurement, which is easier to access, is 98% accurate, and gives a good picture of how your body is structured and whether your muscle mass or fat percentage has changed.

It is very important to emphasize that it can be dangerous to focus on losing body weight as quickly as possible. It is important to respect that a healthy and strong body does not appear overnight. There are no quick-fix solutions that last in the long run. Instead, a strong and healthy body is the result of long-term training and a sustainable diet – with room for living your life and eating cakes too.

IMPORTANT: Consult a healthcare professional to get help if you are over focusing on your weight and body composition.

STRESS AND CALORIE COUNTING

This is a question that comes up often, and you may have thought about it yourself.

Should I count calories to perform optimally on the bike and in everyday life?

The answer is both yes and no, and this requires some explanation.

The quality of the food you eat is far more important than calorie counting. Research shows that the mental strain and effort of counting calories causes stress, fatigue, and burnout, which ultimately results in overeating because you feel controlled and limited[7].

When your body is stressed, the production of cortisol, perhaps better known as the stress hormone, increases. Cortisol affects digestion and the storage processor in the body, which is in no way beneficial in everyday life for humans

When cortisol levels rises, this can inhibit protein synthesis, i.e., the rebuilding of muscles, which happens because the body under stress begins to break down its own stock of protein (muscles) into amino acids and sugar to survive.

Therefore, it will be more difficult to recover and build muscle mass, which is needed to be a strong rider and in daily life.

Having said that, there is a fine balance between measuring and weighing every meal and knowing the nutritional content of the food and ingredients you eat. In regard to the latter, you can easily make the right decisions in terms of judging portions and plate sizes without having to stress yourself out by keeping track of every single calorie. It is therefore important to familiarize yourself with basic nutritional knowledge.

WHAT *should* YOU EAT DURING TRAINING?

How do you know what to eat and when? First, it is important to find out what works for you. Don't try a whole new diet or breakfast on your most important race day. Prepare well in advance by testing different alternatives on your medium and long training rides.

In the end, it's all about you and your personal preferences for taste and consistency when you exercise. Remember that what works for your best friend or the reigning world champion may not necessarily work for you.

Before each training session, it's a good idea to calculate how much energy you will need during your ride and test it repeatedly during training until you get it right. That way, you can be completely ready and sure that you have the proper nutrition planned out for your big competition day.

TIMING OF MEALS
The timing of your meals are important so you can be best prepared for your training or race.

BREAKFAST
During the big races, riders eat a solid breakfast three hours before the start of the race; however, if you leave home early in the morning to get on the bike and hit the roads, you can eat a lighter breakfast an hour before riding out. You must find out how much you need to eat so that you are not too hungry the second you get on the bike; in contrast, you will quickly realize if you have eaten too much too close to the start

of your training. Many northern European riders prefer oatmeal with fruit, honey, or maple syrup for breakfast, with a little protein on the side in the form of eggs or Greek yogurt.

BEFORE A RACE/TRAINING
Eat a small snack, such as a banana or a small piece of cake that is easy to digest, approximately 30 minutes before you get on the bike, to be sure that your glycogen stores are completely full. Many riders also grab a coffee and a visit to the toilet. There is no need to carry unnecessary weight.

DURING TRAINING/RUNNING
The body can store glycogen and keep you going for just over two hours on the bike. If carbohydrates are not added continuously, you will hit the wall or bonk, i.e., run out of energy. It is important to avoid this, as it is close to impossible to recover from bonking whilst you're on the bike. Therefore, it is extremely important to make sure you have enough energy packed in your pockets for the entire trip so that you can get the most out of your training.

> Remember to eat regularly and avoid getting tired and exhausted, especially on trips and exercise longer than an hour.

There are many different recommendations regarding carbohydrate intake during training, some of which go as high as 100-120 g per hour (for trained stomachs and athletes). Not everyone needs that much energy, so try and figure out what works for you.

On long, hard, or demanding stages, it is difficult to consume enough energy through food, cake, and energy bars, so many riders drink a 2:1 mixture of glucose to fructose, as this particular distribution of sugar provides optimal carbohydrate absorption. It is important to emphasize that just ly hydrating you. The sugar content determines whether it is an energy drink or a hydration drink. As a rule of thumb, anything with more than 4% sugar content is not hydrating.

Men can tolerate a higher amount of calories from carbohydrates than women, but women benefit from consuming calories from foods that contain a mix of protein, carbohydrate, and fat to provide optimal energy for their workouts. As a woman, you are less likely to feel bloated, gassy, and uncomfortably full during long workouts if you combine protein, fat, and carbohydrate.

Below, you will find a guide for intake based on the length of your training.

SHORT TRAINING SESSIONS
Duration: Under one hour.
Focus: Hydration.
Fluid: Grand Tour hydration or a low-carb electrolyte drink mix.
Fuel: Your glycogen stores need to be filled up from the start of the day, which means you need to be able to perform without eating anything during a 60-minute training session.

It's always a good idea to bring a small energy bar or banana in case your workout is unexpectedly extended.

MEDIUM TRAINING SESSIONS
Duration: 1–3 hours.
Focus: Carbohydrate intake.
Fluid: Two bottles of low-carb electrolyte drink (depending on the weather, you may need to bring more).
Fuel: Women: 30–60 g / Men 60–90 g of carbohydrate from food/cake per hour (total approx. 120–240 kcal).

LONG TRAINING SESSIONS
Duration: 3+ hours.
Focus: Carbohydrate and electrolyte replenishment and getting enough energy.
Challenge: Reduced desire to eat/lack of appetite.
Fluid: At least two or three bottles of low-carb hydration drink with electrolytes.
Fuel: Women: 30–60 g / Men 60–90 g.

It becomes more difficult for the stomach to digest what you eat as the rides get longer, so eat more solid food and cake at the beginning of the ride, and switch to energy bites and other easily digestible foods during the last part of the trip, e.g., my Race Cakes.

WHAT TO EAT DURING A TRAINING SESSION?
There are many choices when it comes to choosing the right nutrition for your training. Fortunately, there are a lot of great options in this book that you can easily adapt to your personal taste. But first, let's get an overview of what options you have.

Cake
Baked energy bars
Race cakes
Rice bars
Raw bars
Soft sandwiches
Bananas
Homemade energy bites
Energy products of good quality

WHAT ABOUT GELS?
Now, you might be thinking, "What about gels? I see the professional riders and runners swallowing gels all the time. If it's good for them, it must be good for me."

A standard gel pack ranges from 100–120 calories per serving portion. There are typically about 33–40 g of carbohydrates in a package, which consists of maltodextrin and fructose with some sodium, potassium, flavoring, and preservatives.

If you read the nutrition label on the gel, you will see that most instructions say that a gel should be consumed with 60–120 ml of water. This is because gels are very high in concentrated carbohydrate, and if you don't drink enough water on the side, it can't pass through the stomach and into your gut to be absorbed for energy. This means that your body has to draw fluid from its own fluid reserves to dilute the gel so that you can get the energy out of it, ultimately dehydrating you and lowering your performance. Gels contain a mixture of carbohydrates that can overload the transport receptors in your gut, and you can end up with what is known in English as "goo gut" – bloating, flatulence, diarrhea, nausea, and general gastrointestinal discomfort. You don't want to go there.

CAN YOU FUEL ON FAT ALONE?

When the body runs out of energy from glycogen stores, the body switches to burning fat as the primary energy source. This is the body's survival reaction if there is no more food, and it is, for several reasons, in no way optimal for a rider who has to perform.

But what exactly happens for the body to run on fat energy?

In order for the body to convert fat into sugar (energy), it must go through a process called gluconeogenesis, which can be translated as the "new formation of glucose." This is the body's way of ensuring that we can still function even if we don't have any more powder in the fast tank, i.e., energy from carbohydrates. It is also the body's way of ensuring survival if we do not get food for long periods of time, that is, if we are starving.

Gluconeogenesis is a process that can convert protein (in the form of amino acids) and fat (in the form of glycerol) into new glucose molecules, i.e., sugar, which the body can then use as energy. "It's brilliant," you think. "Can't I just run without carbs all the time to burn fat?" The answer is no,

at least if you don't want to break down your muscle mass at the same time.

In order for the body to go through the fat burning process, as mentioned above, protein must be present, which is always the case with your muscle mass. On top of that, it is a longer process for the body to form energy from fat and protein, which requires serious training and adaptation for a rider, since you sit on the bike for many hours, whereas a cross fitter or weightlifter has shorter training sessions. A study has shown that long-distance athletes' "peak power," i.e., the highest number of watts measured during training, was 7% lower in athletes whose primary energy source was fat than in those whose primary energy source came from carbohydrates[9].

RECOVERY

This is important, as it is in the recovery process that all your hard work really pays off.
After training, preferably within a 30-minute window, consume a combination of protein - to give the body the buinding blocks it needs to repair muscle - and carbohydrate to replenish glycogen stores. If you miss this time window, your recovery will not be optimal – your muscles may be very sore the next day, and you will not get the most out of the training you have done.

Aim for 20–25 g of protein as part of your recovery meal, which can either be a shake, leftovers from a rice dish with chicken the day before, a sandwich, or something similar.

HYDRATION

There is no way around the fact that hydration is essential to be able to perform optimally – not only on the bike but also in everyday life in general.

Many of us are slightly dehydrated most of the time, and it affects us more than you might think.

The first sign of dehydration is thirst, and then comes headaches, fatigue, and the inability to focus, making it difficult to perform both on the bike or at work or school. Dehydration affects us cognitively and physically and can negatively impact many body and brain functions:

- Cognitive performance and the ability to focus
- Short-term memory
- Verbal presentation and spelling
- The ability to solve simple problems
- Reaction time and overview
- Eye–hand coordination and motor skills
- Spatial understanding
- Emotional stability
- Increased production of stress hormones

Hydration and water absorption are essential to perform on the bike; it sounds crazy, but water is not enough to keep you hydrated during exercise. Dehydration must be taken very seriously as it can destroy your performance quickly and effectively.

There are many good hydration products on the market. Look for those with a low sugar content (between 2–3.5%) and without artificial sweeteners (which negatively affect the intestinal system). Then, you are guaranteed optimal fluid balance.

The main electrolytes for optimal fluid absorption that you find in many sports drinks on the market are sodium, potassium, magnesium, and calcium.

Sodium (salt) helps maintain fluid balance in the body and attracts fluids to the intestinal system so that they can be absorbed.

Potassium regulates the functioning of the nervous system and helps control muscle contractions and heartbeat.

Magnesium is involved in muscle function and tension control and can affect the fluid balance in the body.

Calcium contributes to muscle function and is necessary for normal nerve function.

WHAT HAPPENS IF I ONLY DRINK WATER?
On very short bike rides of less than an hour, you can easily stick to water, but if you are going on longer rides, you have to prioritize differently. If the liquid (water) you drink does not contain sodium (salt) in the correct amount, it all starts to go wrong.

If you drink too much water, you can experience a condition called hyponatremia, where the sodium concentration in the blood becomes too low. Low sodium content in the blood can lead to water flowing into the cells, thereby diluting the concentration of sodium. When the fluid content is too high in the cells, the body will try to restore the sodium balance by removing excess fluid. The kidneys filter the blood and remove excess fluid, electrolytes, and waste products, which are then excreted from the body through the urine, and the more you urinate, the thirstier you become. Every time you drink more water, the fluid content in the cells becomes higher and higher, and the kidneys will continue to remove more fluid, resulting in an increased amount of urine production and even more thirst. Hyponatremia can result in serious consequences, such as headache, fatigue, convulsions, fainting, coma, and even death.

It's important to note that your fluid and sodium needs can vary depending on your activity level, the weather, your health, and other factors. So, to optimize your workout or training, be smart and do your homework.

CAN YOU HAVE TOO MUCH SODIUM?
Yes, you can. It can happen as a result of too little fluid intake, too much salt intake both through food or salt tablets, or when the body loses too much fluid through sweat, vomiting, or diarrhea. This can lead to severe dehydration as sodium pulls fluid out of the cells and causes an imbalance between the fluid inside and outside the cells. Too much sodium in the blood is called hypernatremia (not to be confused with hyponatremia).

Symptoms of hypernatremia include thirst, headache, lethargy, nausea, and vomiting, and in severe and rare cases, it can lead to seizures, coma, and even death. Death again? Don't worry – we are talking extremes here.

CAN I HAVE A SODA?
All drinks with a high sugar content affect the body's ability to absorb fluid. When the sugar content becomes too high, it is more difficult for the body to absorb and retain the liquid, which can lead to dehydration (instead of hydrating the body) because the high sugar levels also increase urine production and thereby lead to further fluid loss.

WHAT ABOUT ARTIFICIALLY SWEETENED DRINKS?
As a starting point, you should stick to natural and not chemically produced ingredients (such as artificial sweeteners).

Artificial sweeteners come in many varieties, but the most common are sugar alcohols, aspartame, and acesulfame-K. They are often found in zero-calorie sports drinks and energy and protein bars and can cause digestive problems for some people.

Consumption of sugar alcohols such as xylitol, mannitol, and sorbitol can lead to osmotic diarrhea; they have a laxative effect because they are osmotically active and cannot be absorbed in the intestines. When they reach the large intestine, they absorb fluid, which increases the fluid volume of the stool, thereby causing diarrhea. Sugar alcohols can also promote the production of gas in the gut, which can result in bloating and abdominal pain.

Aspartame and acesulfame-K are sweeteners that are often used in diet soft drinks and factory-produced foods. Neither sweetener contributes positively to fluid absorption or optimal performance. In the end, you have to decide for yourself what you want to consume, just remember that everything you consume can ultimately affect your performance.

WHAT DOES IT *take*
TO COMPLETE A TOUR DE FRANCE?

The Tour de France is one of the world's toughest and most demanding sports events, covering around 3,500 kilometers each year, divided over 21 stages, and with only two rest days during those crazy three weeks.

The route varies considerably from stage to stage, with a mix of stages that are relatively flat, hilly, or downright mountainous. The number of calories a rider burns will vary depending on each stage and the individual's size, body composition and shape, and the intensity and duration of their effort. On average, a professional cyclist burns between 5,000 and 8,000 calories a day during the Tour de France, so there needs to be proper fuel in the system to get to the finishing line in Paris.

To bring this further into focus, here are some extreme examples. If we go with the average of 5,000 kcal and 8,000 kcal, which is 6,500 kcal, and we expect riders to burn around 3,500 kcal on a rest day, when they go for a short walk or otherwise relax, the calculation looks like this:

21 stages x 6,500 kcal + two rest days x 3,500 kcal = 143,500 kcal in total

This would correspond to eating:
40 kg of uncooked spaghetti
100 kg of cooked penne without sauce
86 kg of raw chicken breast without skin (approx. 614 pieces)
41 kg of gummy bears
435 kg of broccoli
388 l of lager or beer
20 kg of butter
39 kg of oatmeal
2,050 whole eggs

It is, of course, completely unrealistic to complete a Tour de France race on one of the "diets" above, and I do not recommend trying this at home.

THE BASIC essentials
IN MY KITCHEN

Must haves in the kitchen? Well, here are some basic elements you will always find in my kitchen:

CANNED ITEMS
Peeled tomatoes
Tomato paste
Cornichons
Capers
Dijon mustard
Olives
Tahini
Honey
Maple syrup
Chickpeas and beans

HERBS AND SPICES
Flake salt
Sea salt
Dried oregano
Dried tarragon
Dried basil
Dried thyme
Bay leaves
Curry mix in powder form
Ground coriander
Turmeric
Ginger
Sweet paprika
Smoked paprika
Ground cumin
Ground cloves
Ground cinnamon
Cinnamon sticks
Cardamom
Allspice
Star anise

Nutmeg
Five spice
Dry yeast
Baking soda

DRY ITEMS
Quinoa
Brown rice
Basmati rice
Dried beans
Dried chickpeas
Pasta in various forms
(preferably whole grain)
Gluten-free pasta
Buckwheat noodles
Rice noodles
Sunflower seeds
Pumpkin seeds
Sesame seeds
Hazelnuts
Almonds
Pistachios
Nori seaweed
Dried fruit

OIL AND VINEGAR
Virgin olive oil
Coconut fat (flavored/unflavored)
Hazelnut oil
White wine vinegar
Red wine vinegar
Apple cider vinegar
Balsamic vinegar
Sherry vinegar
Variety of vinegars of different flavors:
raspberry, elderflower, tarragon, etc.

BASIC KITCHEN EQUIPMENT

Scan the code here to read more about fantastic equipment and tools for the kitchen!

Fine grater
Japanese Mandolin
Food processor
Mini chopper
Peeler
Whisk
Rubber spatula
Pepper mill
Salad spinner
Metal spatula

Chef's knife
Utility knife
Paring knife
Cake tester
Knife sharpener
Food thermometer
Small frying pan (20 cm)
Large frying pan (26–30 cm)
Various size pots

IMPORTANT:
– READ THIS BEFORE COOKING!

In order to get the best result, it is important that you read this section and follow the instructions in the recipes every time you try a new one. Remember that recipes are guidelines, and there are many factors that can play a role in how the result turns out when it's ready to serve. It could be a game changer if you don't read the recipe before cooking.

1. READ THE COMPLETE RECIPE!
Yes, it sounds logical, but there are many people who do not read the recipe through before they start cooking, and they will get into trouble (I know you're clearly not one of them.). If you read the recipe from A to Z before starting, you will know what to do and what equipment and ingredients you need. I say this just to be safe, but it helps a lot in the cooking process.

2. SEASON AS YOU COOK!
In the recipes, I write "seasoning" or "taste with salt and pepper regularly," but remember that it is your responsibility to taste and season constantly and before serving, even if it is not noted at each point. By continuously tasting and seasoning as you go, you ensuree a delicious and tasty result.

3. USE QUALITY PRODUCTS!
Your dish is only as good as the ingredients you use. Don't forget that when shopping for groceries.

4. COMMON SENSE!
When you throw yourself into a recipe, you must, of course, remember to use your common sense. Fresh ingredients change throughout the season,

so you have to take into account whether it's a brand-new, young potato or an old, shriveled one. The cooking times and taste will vary accordingly. Young, tender vegetables must be cooked for a shorter time than coarse winter vegetables. If a vegetable isn't tender when the cooking time is up, then it needs something more; it's your responsibility to adjust accordingly.

5. THERE IS ENOUGH FOOD!
It's just your job as the chef to make sure there is enough food at the dinner table. All recipes are created using regular standard serving portion sizes for regular people who do not ride the Tour de France; therefore, it is your responsibility to follow point one and then assess how hungry you are at home and how many people you feed. If the house is full of hungry top athletes, you must adjust the quantities in the recipe. If you or the family are planning a long training session for the day, you must adjust your carbohydrate intake accordingly.

6. SUBSTITUTIONS:
You can substitute most ingredients in the book, just use your common sense.
Any dairy product can be swapped for a plant based version. Vegetables can be swapped for similar type vegetables e.g. Carrot for parsnip, Onion for leek, Nuts for seeds etc. Don't substitute celeriac for green asparagus and strawberries for pine seeds - you get the draft.

7. LAST BUT NOT LEAST!
Enjoy your food. Ps. You can find more great tips on cooking on my website hannahgrant.com

INFORMATION
about THE RECIPES

Scan the code here to read more about nutritional calculations for all recipes.

All the recipes are for approximately four people, unless otherwise stated. The recipes are accompanied with symbols to indicate that they are:

(G) GLUTEN FREE

(N) NUT FREE

(D) DAIRY FREE

(V) PLANT-BASED

IMPORTANT INFORMATION ABOUT THE SYMBOLS IN RELATION TO THE RECIPES:

1. Certain recipes contain nuts, gluten, and dairy products. They are therefore not accompanied by any symbol.

2. At the back of the book, there is a complete alphabetical overview of which recipes are gluten free, nut free, and/or dairy free.

3. Recipes that contain pine nuts, sunflower seeds, and/or sesame seeds are considered nut free, as it is different from nut-allergic to nut allergic whether one can tolerate it or not.

4. Recipes that contain nut oil are not considered nut free.

5. Recipes that contain coconut (coconut milk or coconut oil) are not considered nut free.

6. Recipes in which you can either use dairy products or plant-based alternatives are included as recipes without dairy products, as you can decide for yourself.

7. Recipes that contain soy are included as gluten free, but it depends on which soy you prefer. Read the fine print on the label carefully (tamari is always gluten free).

8. Plant-based recipes are without meat or eggs but may contain dairy products, which you can replace with plant-based products.

9. No account has been taken of the fact that there may be traces of nuts in chocolate.

10. Be aware that some recipes require you to start the day before.

STAGE 1

Easy

 4 people

 15 minutes

BRUSCHETTA *with*
PEA PUREE, MINT, AND LEMON

N V

1 shallot
1 tbsp. butter
1/2 bunch mint
200 g peas, fresh or frozen
4 slices sourdough bread
(regular or gluten-free)
100 g cottage cheese
Juice and zest of 1 lemon
Salt and pepper to taste
1 tbsp. olive oil

1. Peel the onion and chop it finely.
2. Pick the mint, setting some aside for the garnish.
3. Melt the butter in a saucepan and sauté the onion until soft and translucent.
4. Add the peas (setting a few aside for the garnish), season with salt, and cook for 1 minute or until the peas are warm and still beautifully green.
5. Blend the pea mixture in a mini chopper with the mint, cottage cheese, and finely grated lemon zest and season with salt, pepper, and lemon juice.
6. Toast or grill the bread slices and top them with the pea puree.
7. Serve the delicious bruschetta topped with some peas, mint, and lemon zest.

TIP: *Replace the cottage cheese with ricotta.*
Serve with a large green salad.
Add chili flakes on top for a spicy punch.

Easy 4 servings

 20 minutes

PASTA MARINARA
(N) (V) WITH *fresh* TOMATOES

Pasta marinara

500 g dried pasta
1 onion
2 garlic cloves
2 cans peeled tomatoes (2 × 330 g)
1 tin tomato paste (40 g)
1 tbsp. dried oregano
1 bouillon cube
200 ml water
1 tbsp. olive oil

Caprese

200 g fresh cherry tomatoes
2 tbsp. balsamic vinegar
1 tsp. liquid honey or sugar
1 bunch fresh basil
2 tbsp. olive oil
1 mozzarella
Salt and pepper to taste

1. Peel and finely chop the onion and garlic.
2. Heat 1 tbsp. olive oil in a pan and sauté the onion and garlic until tender over medium-high heat.
3. Add the dried herbs and tomato paste. Cook for 1–2 minutes. Add the water and peeled tomatoes. Bring everything to a boil over medium-high heat and then turn down the heat and let simmer. Add half of the basil leaves to the sauce and let simmer for 10–15 minutes while the rest of the dish is being prepared.
4. Bring a pot of salted water to boil for the pasta. Cook the pasta al dente according to the instructions on the bag.
5. Cut the fresh tomatoes into bite-size pieces and toss them with the balsamic vinegar, honey, salt, and pepper. Break the mozzarella into bite-size pieces.
6. Cook the pasta as directed on the packaging.
7. Blend the tomato sauce with the pasta and season with salt and pepper.
8. Drain the fresh tomatoes from the balsamic marinade.
9. Strain the pasta, toss it with half of the sauce and the fresh tomatoes, and heat for 30–45 seconds. Place in bowls and top with the rest of the fresh basil and the mozzarella.

TIP: *Add capers to the sauce. Make extra sauce and keep it in the freezer for a rainy day.*

Easy

 4 people

 15 minutes

PORK CHOPS
with PLUMS AND GREEN HERB SAUCE

(G) (D) (N)

4 pork chops, approx. 2 cm thick

1 bunch basil

1 bunch fresh parsley

1 garlic clove

1 tbsp. capers

50 g olives

3 plums (not too ripe)

3 anchovies

75 ml olive oil

Juice and zest of 1 lemon

Salt and pepper to taste

1. Pick all the herbs. Peel and finely grate the garlic.
2. Cut the plums into thin strips.
3. Chop all the ingredients, except the pork chops, plums, and lemon, with a mini chopper or by hand.
4. Season the herb sauce with salt, pepper, lemon zest, and lemon juice.
5. Heat the oil in a pan. Season the pork chops with salt and pepper and fry them for about 2 minutes on each side.
6. Remove the pork chops from the pan and let rest for a few minutes.
7. Stir-fry the plums in the pan for 1–2 minutes.
8. Mix the plums and the caper mixture together and season with salt, pepper, and lemon.
9. Serve the pork chops topped with the green herb sauce.

TIP: *Serve the chops as part of the stage menu or with a carbohydrate of your choice (e.g., gnocchi, pasta, roasted potatoes, or rice).*
Add dried chili. Make it plant-based: Replace pork chops with tofu.

Easy

 2-3 servings

 10 minutes

HOULE FUEL CHICKEN *and*

Ⓖ Ⓓ MANGO SALAD

Salad

300 g cold cooked chicken

400 g cooked brown rice

1 mini romaine (loose leaf, butterhead, or whatever variety you prefer)

1 mango

1 red onion

1 lime

1 tbsp. maple syrup

150 g small tomatoes

50 g roasted peanuts

1/2 bunch mint

1/2 bunch fresh cilantro or Thai basil

Houle fuel 1.0 dressing

2 tbsp. fish sauce

2 tbsp. soy sauce

2 tbsp Maple sirup

Juice and zest of 1 lime

1/2 tsp. finely grated ginger

1. Cut the chicken into slices.
2. Rinse the lettuce and break it into bite-size pieces.
3. Cut the mango into cubes.
4. Peel the red onion and cut it into thin slices. Marinate the slices in the lime juice and maple syrup.
5. Rinse the tomatoes and cut them into slices.
6. Chop the peanuts.
7. Mix the dressing and toss it together with all the ingredients. Season with salt and lime juice.
8. Plate the salad in bowls and top with the roasted peanuts and fresh herbs.

STIR FRY NOODLES *with*

(G) BEEF AND GREENS

400 g rice noodles

200 g beef diced or sliced
(go with your favorite cut)

2 bok choy

200 g broccoli

2 red onions

50 ml soy sauce

1 tsp. toasted sesame oil

2 tbsp. roasted peanuts

1/2 bunch mint

2 tbsp. oil for frying

1. Bring a pot of salted water to a boil.
2. Cook the noodles according to the instructions on the package and then let drain while you prepare the other ingredients.
3. Peel the red onion. Cut it in half and slice it lengthwise.
4. Rinse the bok choy and broccoli. Cut the bok choy into wedges and the broccoli into bite-size pieces.
5. Pick the mint leaves and roughly tear them.
6. Coarsely chop the peanuts.
7. Heat 1 tbsp. oil in a pan. Season the beef with salt and pepper and fry it for 1–2 minutes. Then, let the meat rest on a plate.
8. Wipe the pan and heat it well with 1 tbsp. oil. Roast the broccoli and red onion for approx. 2 minutes. Season with salt and pepper.
9. Blanch the bok choy for 10–12 seconds in boiling water, drain.
10. Throw the noodles on the pan and fry them for 1 minute.
11. Add the soy sauce and toasted sesame oil. Stir in the vegetables and meat.
12. Arrange the noodles in bowls and top with chopped peanuts and mint.

TIP: *Replace the beef with chicken or pork. You can also use leftover sliced or diced meats.*

RACE *cakes* WITH CHERRIES

Ⓖ Ⓓ Ⓥ

300 g baked sweet potato
(bake until tender with the skin on at
200 °C/390 °F for approx. 45–50 minutes)

4 eggs

65 g oatmeal

2 tbsp. almond flour

6 dates

2 tbsp. firm honey

1/2 vanilla pod

1 tsp. cardamom

2 tsp. baking soda

Zest and juice of 1 lemon

1/2 tsp. salt

75 g melted butter

30 g cherries, fresh or frozen

2 tbsp. almond flour (for the tins)

1. Preheat the oven to 170°C/340°F.
2. Blend all the ingredients, except for the butter and cherries.
3. Add the melted butter to the mixture while blending on low to medium speed.
4. Flavor the batter with more cinnamon, lime zest, and/or honey to your taste.
5. Grease the muffin tins and sprinkle them with almond flour. If you use paper cups, you can sprinkle a little coconut flour on the bottom.
6. Rinse the cherries if using fresh cherries.
7. Use a spoon to fill the tins/paper cups with batter and press the cherries gently into the batter. Depending on the size of the tins/cups and how much batter you fill them with, the baking time will vary. There should be around 2.5–3 cm of batter in each tin/cup.
8. Bake the cakes for approx. 25 minutes in a hot air oven or 30 minutes in a traditional oven. Rotate the muffin tins once or twice during baking time to ensure even baking.
9. The cakes are ready when they are golden brown and firm.

NOTE: *You can replace the cherries with pretty much any fruit: plums, peaches, pears, etc. Use your imagination!*
If the dates are dry, add 50–100 ml of water to the batter.

HUGO HOULE

Pro rider since 2011

Hugo Houle began racing triathlons as a boy but opted for road cycling as a teenager and later became a skilled pro rider. The Canadian has done seven grand tours and is a Tour de France stage winner.

"I was born in 1990 in Quebec, a French-speaking part of Canada. I was raised in Sainte-Perpétue, a small village with about 1000 inhabitants, more or less, and that's where I lived most of my life before I left home for cycling. My parents moved from there a few years ago, but it was mostly stable growing up in that small village where there were a lot of coal fields and agriculture around, mainly fields. So that's where I began riding my bike, and most of the time, I fell completely flat, like a pancake."

He is neither the first nor the last cyclist to have heard as a youngster that he had too much energy and should expend some of it. So he did.

"I always knew I loved the bike as a kid, playing outside and building jump-in woods with ramps so my friends and I could jump high. Growing up, I was more into the BMX style of bikes. And then, I would say, around 10 or 11 years old, I started triathlons with my brother, which was an idea my mom proposed to get us to exert our extra energy because we were a bit turbulent at school. So that is how I started and continued until I was 16 years old when I got better at cycling, so I switched to road cycling. I think I've always had the desire to win and have always wanted to be better, so that thought pushed me to grow at every step of my journey. And in 2011, I had my first professional contract with SpiderTech, a Canadian team. And

then in 2013, I went to AG2R La Mondiale, a French team, for five years; Astana for four years; and now to Israel-Premier Tech."

As a pro rider, he is now very focused on food and nutrition, but it was not always like that in the early years of his career.

"When I started, it was different. What we knew about nutrition then is nothing compared to what we do today. When I was younger, I thought that because I was training, I could eat whatever I wanted to. I spent energy, so I needed energy. I was not, in any way, calculating what I ate. So, for me, there was no diet or anything special. I ate more cake, which was definitely my favorite. I have a sweet tooth, which I still have today. The lack of a diet plan made me gain much weight easily in the off-season. So, over the years, I've learned that diet is important when it comes to my weight, but in the beginning, I just didn't really care. I was just eating a lot."

"And there was no information available or particular attention paid to how many calories were in the carbohydrates or vegetables I ate. I mean, all we ate was basically what my mom cooked, and that was it. Of course, we use a lot of carb-rich maple syrup from where I grew up, which was close to the tree fields, and it's especially good in cakes, but you can use it in many things."

As an adult, he learned to cook and still enjoys cooking today. He usually does the cooking at home during the off-season, and a typical day for Hugo Houle food-wise looks like this, he says.

"For my basic breakfast, I eat oatmeal, which I try to do differently most of the time, but my go-to recipe is to have bananas inside it. I make the oatmeal mixture with water and add milk to make it more creamy."

"If I have a bigger day, then I can have some dates and stuff. I kind of adjust it according to the training I'm going to do and how much I want to eat, but 80% of the time, I will have oats topped with fresh blueberries and raspberries and a little bit of my homemade granola with maple syrup and a bit of cinnamon. This meal gives me the energy that fuels my training on the bike, depending on the training or whatever, but I still like to have something I made myself, like a cake or raisins. But, yeah, or banana bread; I just always have some cake I eat while training; it can also be a muffin as long as it fits easily in my pocket. I start the ride with the food that I cook. And then, on the day of the long ride, I will finish with a typical gel to ensure I am good and have constant power that keeps me more in control."

It's all about carbs after training to recover quickly and effectively. He heads back home, enters the kitchen, and begins cooking.

"I keep my meal after training quite simple, depending on what I have in the fridge. But mainly, the base would be rice or pasta. And then, depending on what I have, like if I have any chicken left or some vegetables, I can crack an egg on my rice and maybe make a soy sauce, quick pot rice, which is basically the snack after the race. In winter, I like to have soup because it's cold, and even in the south, but still, in the mountains, we always find a way to get cold. So I do more like a puree with the vegetable I have left, whatever, or with sweet potato or other stuff inside. Depending on what I have leftover."

Hugo Houle's strategy for fueling up changes at dinner time as he plans for future training sessions and counts his carbs intake.

"Dinner will be the part where, depending on what I'm going to do the next day, I will adapt what I'm going to eat. So, if I'm not training a lot, I will eat more salad, more vegetables with protein, and a good portion of protein at night. And if I have a big training day coming up, I will maybe eat pasta or whatever. I count my carbs

at dinner. If not, I eat too much and just don't get where I need to go. So, I feel like this method works well for me. A nutritionist taught me this, completely changing how I perform. I began to notice the difference when I started, and since then, I've never looked back; I think that was around 2018 – historic already. And then I developed an efficient way of eating and maintaining my calories with him."

In his team, riders have access to a nutritionist, and Hugo Houle is no exception. He takes advice but, at the same time, finds his way. He says weighing and calculating food and nutrition are gradually becoming a thing at most teams.

"I would be surprised to see a teammate without scales unless the food was pre-weighed. That's the standard now; two or three years ago, if you tried something like that, they'd look at you like an extraterrestrial; you were kind of special if you used the scale, but now the team provides it to all teammates."

"I prefer a Bluetooth scale with my phone, so nobody sees me weighing my food. If I go to a typical buffet restaurant, I just put my scale under the plate, drop the plate, put the rice that I want or whatever, and then see; then I have an Excel sheet on my phone to calculate everything on my phone. So I just use my phone as the Excel sheet, and then I enter what I will eat, and I get a total of carbs, depending on what I put in, but the system of the nutritionists who taught me that you could manage yourself, that you don't always need to call him or whatever, makes it easy for you."

After a long day on the road, eating lots of food is not only for fuel and recovery, he says. It is also very important for morale and mood.

"For sure. It has always been like this for me; I do so much sport, and it's a gift that I can eat more. I mean, even if I calculate and watch everything, eating enough on the Grand Tour before the big days is a challenge. You can eat a lot, and it's nice. And it's really nice for us as cyclists to have a chef on board, which certainly changed our lives. Because before my team had a chef, my teammates and I would go to a hotel, and we would get white pasta because it was too hard to find anything that was good, still fresh, and that you could trust. But now we get good-quality food, which leaves us in a better mood and increases our recovery time. We eat different things every day, and they taste good. It is just more enjoyable to have a chief. And you can see the outcome. I mean, if you go from eating only white rice with tuna for 21 days in a Grand Tour, which was the case for my teammates and me two or three years ago because that was the only thing we had, to getting a chief, you will definitely notice the changes. It is just more fun, and as you said, when you have a bad day on the bike or a long day, you are compensated for that with a warm meal. That is good, and then, yeah, it kind of makes you happy, and you go to bed way better, and the hotel doesn't matter so much when we have the chef with us. I mean, we used to get really sad when we got in some hotels."

Food at the big races is not only about quality or big plates with mountains of food for fueling up. Timing is essential, Hugo Houle says.

"The way you manage your carbs is the key to your performance. I would say the source and timing of it are important; timing is the key."

"It used to be common for guys to train without eating in order to become more efficient at burning fat and stuff. Recent studies show that you have to eat while on the bike. I mean how you manage your carbs; that's the key to achieving your desired goals. For example, if you have a big training day the next day, you should have a nice dinner with a reliable source of carbs the night before. And then, in the morning, three hours before you leave, the basic rule is to have some good oats or whatever source of carbs you prefer. Currently, many guys eat oats more than in the past. Having a good portion of carbs is essential to your performance when you train hard. If you want to go lighter on your training, it is better when the ride is slow because if you don't have enough energy, you won't be able to push yourself enough in your training. You need to ensure you have the right carbs per hour."

In order to get the right amount of carbs per hour, you need to do a bit of counting and planning, no matter if you are an amateur or a pro rider. Amounts may vary, but planning will boost the value of training.

"Let's say someone takes between 60 and 90 grams of carbs before going hard on training; he might become fat in the long run. I will not recommend that anyone train while eating 90 grams of carbs beforehand everyday; if you do an hour of full gas on the climb, then don't hesitate to take up to 90 grams of carbs; professionally, we do way more than that."

"But for normal people, I think it's enough. But yeah, basically eat, but not too much, and drink enough, as what most drink companies sell us is way higher in carbs than before. Previously, drinks used to contain way more electrolytes, but drinks are becoming a big game changer for carb intake. If you can get 100 grams of carbs in one bottle, It's like three to four gels in the past. Can you imagine having four gels in one hour? Well, you can now smash this drink in one hour. But this is where we're headed."

STAGE

Easy

 2-4 servings

 10 minutes

SAUTEED GREENS

(G) (D) (V) *with* CASHEWS

400 g bok choy or fresh spinach
3 garlic cloves
25 g roasted cashews
2 tbsp. olive oil
2 tbsp. soy sauce
2 tbsp. toasted sesame oil
Salt to taste

1. Rinse and drain the bok choy.
2. Peel the garlic and cut it into thin slices.
3. Coarsely chop the cashews.
4. Heat olive oil in a large sauté pan over low-medium heat. Roast the garlic until it is golden brown at the edges. Season with a little salt.
5. Toss in the bok choy, add the soy sauce and sesame oil, and cover. Shake the pan and let the bok choy steam through for approx. 10–15 seconds. Toss until all of the bok choy is cooked.
6. Season with salt and arrange on a plate. Top with roasted cashews.

TIP: *You can use all types of leafy greens, such as spinach or beets. Just remember that the cooking time is shorter if you're just using leaves.*

BAKED *sweet* POTATO

GOAT CHEESE CREME AND DUKKAH

(G) (V)

1 large sweet potato
200 g soft fresh goat cheese
100 ml Greek yogurt
Juice and zest of 1 lemon
100 g hazelnuts, shelled
50 g sesame seeds
1 tsp. coriander seeds
1 tsp. cumin, whole
1/2 bunch dill
Salt and pepper to taste
Olive oil

1. Preheat the oven to 170°C/340°F.
2. Cut the sweet potato into quarters lengthwise.
3. Place on a baking sheet lined with baking paper, cut side up. Brush with a little olive oil and season with salt and pepper. Bake for 45–50 minutes or until completely tender.
4. On a dry pan at medium heat, toast the nuts, sesame, coriander seeds, and cumin until it smells delicious. Cool and grind into a granule in a mini chopper. Season to taste with salt.
5. Combine the goat cheese and yogurt and season with salt, pepper, and lemon zest and juice.
6. Arrange the sweet potato on a plate, topped with the goat cheese crème, dukkah, a little olive oil, and fresh dill.

TIP: *Serve the dish cold or hot.*
You can replace the goat cheese with another type of fresh cheese, such as ricotta or mascarpone or use crumbled feta. You can also refrain from using cheese completely, then just season the yogurt. Top with fresh herbs to taste.

PAN FRIED COD
WITH *tangy* SALSA

500–600 g cod fillet
2 limes, juice and zest
1 red onion
1/2 mild green chili
1 small garlic clove
1 green pepper
1 large tomato
1/2 bunch coriander
2 tbsp. olive oil
Salt and pepper to taste

1. Divide the cod into 4 equal pieces. Season with salt and pepper and let rest while preparing the salsa.
2. Peel and cut the red onion, pepper, and tomato into chunks.
3. In a mini chopper, blend the red onion with the lime juice and finely grated lime zest from 1 lime. Let the blended onion marinate in the lime juice for 2–3 minutes until it is completely pink.
4. Add the bell pepper, tomato, finely grated garlic, finely chopped chili, and fresh coriander to the onion mix. Season with salt and pepper and use the pulse function to chop into a chunky salsa.
5. Add the olive oil and season with lime juice and zest and salt. Set aside in a bowl.
6. Heat oil in a pan over medium-high heat and fry the fish skin side down for 1–2 minutes or until approx. 80% done. You should be able to see that the edges have browned and that the fish meat has turned white. Carefully flip the fish with a spatula and fry for 10–20 more seconds. Turn off the heat and let the fish finish cooking on the leftover heat from the pan. If the cod piece is very thick, the frying time must be slightly increased.
7. Arrange the fish on a plate and top with salsa.

TIP: *To tell when the fish is ready, use a meat skewer or cake tester to poke through the meat. If the tip slides effortlessly through the fish fillet, the fish is cooked; if it meets resistance, the fish is still raw.*

Easy

 1 large cake or 12 small ones

 60 minutes

WATT THE FUDGE *cake*
CHOCOLATE CAKE WITH CINNAMON FUDGE

(G) (D) (V)

Cake:

200 g diced uncooked sweet potato

3 large eggs

12 pitted Medjool dates (approx. 100 g)

2 tbsp. coconut oil or butter

1 tsp. baking soda

4 tbsp. unsweetened cocoa powder

1/4 tsp. salt

2 tsp. cinnamon

50 g almonds

30 g oatmeal

Cinnamon fudge:

12 pitted Medjool dates

1 tbsp. ground cinnamon

100–200 ml boiling water

40 g melted butter

1/2 tsp. salt

Fresh blueberries for decoration

1. Blend all the cake ingredients into a batter a bit more firm than regular cake batter.
2. Line a cake tin with baking paper or grease it with coconut oil and sprinkle it with nut or oat flour.
3. Fill the cake tin with the batter and make sure to level the surface of the batter with a wet spoon to avoid burned "mountain-tops" during baking.
4. Bake the cake at 170°C/340°F for 40–50 minutes (or approx. 35 minutes if you go for muffins) until golden brown and firm. If the cake feels very soft, then it needs a little longer. Remember to turn the cake once halfway through the baking time.
5. While the cake is baking, make the cinnamon fudge glaze.
6. Let the dates soak for 5 minutes in boiling water. NOTE: If your dates are very dry, you may need to use a little more water and soak them for a little longer.
7. Blend the dates with water, cinnamon powder and salt until smooth. If the dates are very soft, start with 1/3 of the water and then add more of needed.
8. Add a little melted butter at a time to the date mixture and blend at medium speed until smooth. Season with cinnamon and a little more salt to taste and adjust the consistency with a little extra water if necessary.
9. Top the cake with cinnamon fudge and add blueberries before serving.

TIP: *Divide the cake mixture into muffin tins for individual portions and use them for training. You can make them into mini cinnamon fudge sandwiches by placing the filling between two pieces of cake, making them easier to take with you on your bike rides.*

STAGE

Easy

 4-6 people

 60 minutes

 # QUINOA BOWL

300 g quinoa
300 g beetroot
1 large sweet potato
200 g cottage cheese
25 g pistachios
Salt and pepper to taste
1 bunch parsley
Fresh tarragon or dill
Olive oil

1. Preheat the oven to 200°C/390°F.
2. Drizzle the beetroot (leave the skin on) with oil and season with salt. Wrap in aluminum foil.
3. Bake the beetroot for 45–50 minutes until tender.
4. Peel the sweet potato and cut it into 2 × 2 cm cubes. Toss with olive oil, salt, and pepper. Place on a baking tray lined with baking paper and bake in the oven for 25–30 minutes until tender and lightly golden.
5. Rinse and cook the quinoa according to the instructions on the package. Let it sit in the post with a lid for approx. 10 minutes to rest and then let cool.
6. Pour boiling water over the parsley and then squeeze the liquid out of the leaves once cool. Chop the leaves and puree them with a little cold water. Season the puree with salt to taste.
7. Mix the quinoa and parsley puree together and arrange the mixture like small mountaintops in bowls.
8. Season the cottage cheese with salt and pepper to taste.
9. Chop the pistachios.
10. Remove the skin from the beetroots and cut them into bite-size pieces (if possible, use gloves so that your fingers aren't stained).
11. Arrange the beetroot, baked sweet potato and cottage cheese around the quinoa mountains. Top with chopped pistachios and freshly ground black pepper.

▲ Medium   ◎ 4 people

⏱ 40 minutes

CHICKEN *in* TOMATO SAUCE
(G) (N) ## WITH MOZZARELLA

2 onions
2 garlic cloves
2 cans peeled and diced tomato
300 ml water
1 bouillon cube (chicken/veg)
1 tsp. dried tarragon
1 tbsp. dried basil
1 tsp. dried oregano
3 tbsp. olive oil
1 fresh mozzarella ball
1 bunch fresh basil
4 chicken breasts (skin on)
Salt and pepper to taste

1. Preheat the oven to 170°C/340°F.
2. Peel and finely chop the onion and garlic.
3. Heat 2 tbsp. olive oil in a large, oven-proof sauté pan and sauté the onion and garlic until tender.
4. Add the dry spices.
5. Season with salt and pepper and add in the canned tomatoes and water. Bring sauce to a boil and then reduce to a simmer.
6. Cut the mozzarella into eight slices.
7. Pick the basil leaves.
8. With a thin, sharp knife, make a 2-cm deep and 3- to 4-cm-long cut in the side of the chicken breast, where it is thickest. Then, through the cut you just made, cut a pocket inside the breast. Do it carefully so that you don't cut through the breast or your fingers.
9. Place 4–5 basil leaves between two slices of mozzarella. Season with salt and pepper and stuff into the pocket of the chicken breast. you can use the inner filet to close the hole.
10. Season the chicken breasts with salt and pepper and brown them in a pan with 1 tbsp. olive oil over medium-high heat.
11. Place the chicken breasts in the sauce and cook the whole dish in the oven for approx. 25–30 minutes or until the chicken is cooked through but still juicy.
12. Top with basil and serve with pasta, rice, or mashed potatoes.

> **TIP:** *Add cooked chickpeas to the sauce before baking the dish.*
> *You can add more vegetables, e.g., fennel or squash, to the sauce if you want it to be chunkier.*
> *You can omit the cheese and just fill the breasts with lots of fresh herbs, toss them in a little olive oil, and season them with salt and pepper.*

RISOTTO *a la*

(G) (N) ASGREEN

400 g risotto rice
300 ml white wine
1300 ml chicken stock or broth
400 g peas, fresh or frozen
3 onions
2 garlic cloves
Juice and zest of 1 lemon
100 g parmesan
1 bunch chives
2 tbsp. olive oil
Salt and pepper to taste

1. Warm up the chicken stock.
2. Peel and finely chop the onions and garlic.
3. Heat the olive oil in a sauté pan or large pot over medium-high heat and sauté the onions and garlic until tender, without them taking color.
4. Add rice and sauté until covered in olive oil.
5. Pour in the wine and let come to a boil, stirring constantly.
6. Turn down heat to just below medium, add 200 ml stock to the rice, and cook, stirring constantly, until the liquid is almost completely absorbed. Continue until all the stock has been absorbed and your risotto is soft, creamy, and delicious, with a little bite. It should cook for 17–20 minutes depending on how much bite you want.
7. Add grated Parmesan and season with salt, pepper, lemon zest, and lemon juice.
8. Set the risotto aside.
9. Finely chop the chives thinly.
10. Warm the peas for 30–40 seconds until they are warm, cooked and still beautifully green.
11. Mix half of the peas into the risotto and adjust, if necessary, with a little extra water or stock. The risotto should be so creamy that it flattens out when you shake the serving bowl.
12. Toss the rest of the peas with lemon zest and a little lemon juice and serve in bowls. Optionally, top with a little extra grated parmesan and freshly ground pepper.

TIP: *You can add flavorings, such as thyme, rosemary stalks, saffron, or star anise, to the stock when it cools to give the dish more flavor.*
Serve the dish with fresh green asparagus.

DULCE DE LECHE
cream WITH BAKED PLUMS

(G) (N) (V)

1 can condensed milk
250 ml whipping cream
1 kg plums
50 g rolled oats
6 tbsp. maple syrup
1/2 tsp. cinnamon
1 lime
1/4 tsp. salt

1. To make dulce de leche, Bring the can of condensed milk to a boil in a pot; then, turn heat to low and let the can simmer for 3 hours. The can must always be covered with water. Allow the tin to cool before opening.
2. Preheat the oven to 170°C/340°F.
3. Mix oats, 2 tbsp. of maple syrup, and salt together and spread evenly on a baking tray lined with baking paper.
4. Toast in the oven until crispy and golden, about 15 minutes, and remove to let cool.
5. Turn the oven up to 180°C/355°F.
6. Halve the plums, remove the stones, and toss the plums with 4 tbsp. of maple syrup and the cinnamon.
7. Place the plums in an ovenproof dish with a thin bottom and bake for 15 minutes until they are warm, delicious and fully cooked.
8. Combine 1/4 of the cream with 150 g of the cooled dulce de leche.
9. Then add the rest of the cream and whip it with an electric mixer into a light foam.
10. Arrange the plums and top with dulce de leche cream and crispy oats.

TIP: *If in a hurry, whip the cream with a bit of vanilla and maple syrup instead of dulce de leche.*

"You need it. Eat it."

KASPER ASGREEN

Pro rider since 2018

Kasper Asgreen won the 2021 Tour of Flanders. He was born in 1995 and was 15 years old when he started cycling. He has ridden six seasons as a professional. The Team Sudal Quickstep rider was inspired by watching the Tour de France and joined the local cycling club, Kolding Bicycle Klub.

"I watched the Tour de France on television. Maybe cycling was for me, I thought. After all, it was a time with excellent riders like Cancellara and the Schleck brothers and Contador, who were at the top at the time. It was impossible not to be inspired and motivated."

Diet was not something that he thought about as a young rider in his first races. He fueled up with a true classic.

"I call it a ritual – that portion of pasta with ketchup and ham in the car on the way out to bike races every weekend – a ritual that stayed with me for many years. It's not a delicacy, but it did me good to get some carbohydrates, and it was easy to have with you in a box. Breakfast was oatmeal with milk and a splash of jam. It gave good energy for the trip on the country roads."

Despite his career as a professional rider, Kasper Asgreen does not think much about his weight. He does not have a strict diet but eats when he is hungry. His weight fluctuates within a kilo.

"Whether it's in-season or off-season makes no difference. I eat according to whether I'm hungry or not. When it's off-season, I'm not hungry when I wake up. I rarely eat before lunchtime because I don't exercise at all, so my energy consumption is much lower, and I am still full from the evening meal the day before. If I wake up and I'm not hungry, it's because the body doesn't need anything. My approach is always to just listen to the body. What does the body need? That should speak for itself. That's the way I try to do it."

Not everyone else naturally masters intuitive eating and the ability to feel how the body feels. For Kasper Asgreen, it has always been this way.

"Just because you get up in the morning doesn't mean you have to eat breakfast. There is no reason to eat just to eat."

It changes significantly for him when it is the in-season.

"When the amount of training is turned up, you also get more and more hungry. It is super important to fill up on something before training, for breakfast, when training, and immediately after training. It is the most important meal circle of the day. When the season is underway, it is around training. If you have to adjust the weight, it is typically during the evening meals. Or snacks during the afternoon to get the weight up or down. Before, during, and right after training hours, it is all about fueling up."

On race days before a stage, Kasper Asgreen does not compromise either but consumes an extensive diet.

"Breakfast typically consists of a portion of oatmeal with various dried fruits, [and] honey – something that is reasonably sugary, i.e., carbohydrate rich without filling up too much because it's about filling up a lot for the stage. But it can be difficult – if you eat things that take up a lot in terms of volume – to eat enough down. You feel fueled but are not properly fueled up and ready for the stage."

"So dried fruit, honey, and things like that are mixed into the oatmeal. And then typically some form of protein, and it's often eggs when we have our own chef with us, and if not, then we have to see what's on the hotel menu. Then it can be some yogurt. If not, there are eggs along with two or three pieces of good, big pieces of baguette, or whatever else is made of bread, and then maybe some jam, Nutella, honey, carbo-hydrate, sugary butter, or a kind of spread. It is typically breakfast. And then we get a snack rich in carbs three to three and a half hours before the start. About an hour before the start, we eat some carb cakes that our energy sponsor makes."

After the race or stage, a protein shake, and an extensive carbohydrate-rich meal, typically with rice as the main ingredient, are a must.

"There is usually always white rice in a large rice cooker inside the bus because there are people who just want white rice. And then there are dif-ferent lunch boxes with a rice dish, a pasta dish, a sandwich, a wrap, or something else. When we get to the hotel, they usually have some smoothies ready for us, and you can get a little extra if you feel like it. And then a massage and then down to dinner, which is calculated perso-nally for each rider. We send our individual watt files to the dietitian, who calculates how much carbohydrate and protein we need for the meal, and dinner is arranged based on that data."

After a long stage, riders must eat up and finish their plates. There is no excuse. In fact, eating more than planned is okay as long as you listen to your body's needs, according to Kasper Asgreen.

"The meal provided is our minimum portion, but we are also encouraged that if we are hungrier, we are very welcome to take more. The chef al-ways asks in the morning what we want to eat for dinner. As always, we have two choices: usually a piece of fish or a piece of meat. It can be chick-en, pork, or beef. It can get a bit monotonous because fish is always on the menu, but meat is varied according to which stage it is. If you're going out to do mountain work, you won't just get a heavy piece of pork on your plate in the evening because it will punish you the day after. But if you have a few days where it's relatively flat to get through, then you can get something a little heavier. But if it's a mountain stage, then it's usually fish or chicken for a few days."

Although it can be monotonous, Kasper Asgreen never gets tired of the menu during big stage races like the Tour de France.

"When we are in-season, the food does not become so much a dining experience. It becomes more that it is fuel, and it has to go in."

"So no, I don't get tired of it because it's part of being at a bike race. You need it. Eat it. I know I need carbs, so I cannot complain that there is often rice and pasta. It is just the way it is, and the body needs it if it is to perform."

Kasper Asgreen listens to his body and uses the body's signals as landmarks. That is why he doesn't count calories either.

"No, I do not. I am often in a situation where it is difficult for me to keep the weight up, so it is often something to eat as much as possible and then things that are as calorie dense as possible because otherwise, I can't keep up with anything. Then I lose too much weight. And so it is that du-ring the really heavy training periods, if I don't eat some Haribo, or some kind of candy, or some cake, or some of those things that are unhealthy becau-se they are so calorie dense normally, then I can't keep up. That's part of my stuff, those unhealthy things, and also lots of oil on the pasta and things like that in general that are quite calorie dense. Because otherwise, I lose weight too quickly. So no, I do not count calories. It is more about eating as much as possible because I do not want to lose too much weight. For me, it's not about how much I eat. It is simply a matter of getting enough to eat. I would also like to eat a dessert."

It may sound as if Kasper Asgreen has a magical body and that he can eat whatever he wants. But he points out that you get the furthest by listening to your body. This is also the advice he passes on to young riders: They should have fun with cycling and not get too caught up in exercise and diet plans.

"The most important thing is to keep having fun. I think there are many who fall into the trap of thinking that now it must be super serious. Then they start with diet plans, coaching and training plans, bike fits, and intervals on each workout. It quickly becomes too much. It kills the joy of being a rider."

"I also fell into that trap when I was a U23 rider. There was a season when I was not having fun with it anymore. It wasn't like I was thinking about quitting because I still wanted to hit the road. I was just unmotivated when I had to go out to train. It had become too much, too fast. That's what I fell for – when you come out for joint training and race up the inclines and sprint to the signs. But I didn't do that anymore because now I had the training plan that stages and pulses this and that and this and that. The most important thing is to keep having fun."

"A training plan is only indicative. A diet plan is only indicative. Nothing you do one day is going to change anything. It's what you

do consistently over a long period of time that makes the difference."

It's about striking a balance between the fun and the serious. This applies to the diet and the amount of exercise. There are no standard rules, but it is up to the individual rider to fuel according to their needs.

"It is very individual. What may work for me may not necessarily work for others. But I've always been good at taking my rest days when I needed them, so it has never been an issue for me. I think the most important thing is not to do anything too extreme. There is no reason for that. Be balanced in everything, and do not get too serious about things. When you're young, there must be room to go out and have a beer with your classmates. Obviously, if you are in-season, don't drink a lot of beer. You can still go out and enjoy yourself with your friends and drink one beer. I often think that there are many who become too serious too quickly. Remember to relax a little. It is just sport. It is just exercise."

On the other hand, there is a rule of thumb that Kasper Asgreen does not compromise on. It is a rule that he passes on to younger riders and has no doubts about its importance. It is not about carbohydrates, weight, or sugar but about the will to get out on the roads when it seems easiest to stay at home.

"Remember to go out and ride your bike when it is raining dogs. Fuel up, ride, and endure. It will do you good."

STAGE

Medium

 6 people

1 hour and 20 minutes

RAINBOW TERRINE of ROOT VEGETABLES

(G) (D) (N) (V)

4 carrots
4 beetroots
4 parsley roots
1 large sweet potato
2 red onions
2 eggs
1/4 bunch fresh thyme
7-8 leaves of fresh sage
50 g butter/ coconut oil
Salt and pepper to taste

1. Preheat the oven to 160°C/320°F.
2. Peel all the root vegetables.
3. Using a mandolin slicer or food processor, cut each peeled vegetable into thin slices, keep them separately. Finish with the beetroots, as they will stain the other vegetables.
4. Finely mince the onion. Rinse, pick, and chop the thyme.
5. Melt the butter.
6. Toss each root vegetable with equal parts onion, thyme, and melted butter and season with salt and pepper.
7. Whisk the two eggs together with salt and pepper.
8. Line a baking tin with baking paper. Place the sage leaves on the bottom and then the root vegetables on top in layers: first, the sweet potato, then the beetroot, then the carrot, and then the parsley and sweet potato.
9. Pour in half the beaten eggs after the beetroot layer and the other half after the carrot layer.
10. Cover the baking tin with baking paper and bake for approx. 60 minutes or until a cake tester slides through the vegetables effortlessly. The taller the terrine, the longer the baking time.
11. When it's done, use a flat lid or container to carefully press the terrine together, so that all air holes disappear.
12. If you want to serve the terrine immediately, let it rest for 10–15 minutes and cool before cutting.
13. If you want a perfect serving, let the terrine cool completely in the fridge before cutting into the desired shape. Then, either fry or reheat the terrine slices in the oven.

TIP: *You can wrap cold pieces of terrine in puff pastry and bake them in the oven at 200°C/390°F for 20–25 minutes to make a festive meal. REMEMBER: Puff pastry is not the optimal daily diet for a pro rider.*

Easy

 4-6 people

 5-10 minutes

Green HUMMUS
WITH DUKKAH

Ⓖ Ⓓ Ⓥ

Hummus

2 large handfuls of fresh herbs
(parsley, chives, dill, etc.)
240 g cooked chickpeas (1 can)
100 ml water from the cooked chickpeas
60 g liquid light tahini
2 garlic cloves
1 tsp. cumin
Zest and juice of 1–2 lemons
Salt and pepper to taste
Optional: Small tomatoes for serving

Dukkah

50 g hazelnuts
1 tbsp. whole cumin
1 tbsp. whole coriander seeds
Salt to taste

Small fresh tomatoes

NOTE: When choosing tahini, make sure it is a delicious, light, and creamy version. Some types of tahini can be very bitter.

1. Bring a saucepan of water to a boil. Blanch the fresh herbs in the boiling water for 2 seconds. Shock them in cold water; then, squeeze out any excess water and chop roughly.
2. Blend the herbs into a puree with a little of the water from the chickpeas.
3. Add the chickpeas, tahini, grated garlic, and finely grated lemon zest and juice. Season and adjust the texture with more liquid if necessary.
4. Leave the hummus to rest for 5 minutes. Then, blend and season again with salt, pepper, and more lemon juice to taste.
5. In a dry pan over medium-high heat, toast all ingredients for the dukkah.
6. Once the nuts are golden and smell toasted (not burnt), remove the mixture from the heat, let it cool, and roughly chop it using a mini chopper, a spice grinder, or a mortar. Season to taste with salt.
7. Plate the hummus and top with the dukkah. Serve as a dip with delicious bread or fresh vegetables.

TIP: *You can also make variations of the basic recipe. All ingredients are blended in step 1. Adjust the texture of the hummus and use it as a sauce for your main course.*

Variation with fresh herbs: *1/2 bunch fresh parsley, coriander, or your favorite herb. Pick the herbs and blanch them for a few seconds in boiling water. Cool the herbs in cold water and blend them with the basic recipe above.*

Variation with dried spices: *1 tsp. paprika (preferably smoked), 1/2 tsp. cayenne pepper.*

Variation with Greek yogurt: *100 g Greek yoghurt.*

6-8 pita breads
1 leg of lamb (approx. 1.7-2 kg)

Spice mix
2 tbsp. ground black pepper
1 tsp. crushed cloves
1/2 tsp. crushed cardamom
1 tsp. fennel seeds
1 tsp. caraway seeds
1 tsp. ground cumin
1 tbsp. grated nutmeg
1 tsp. ground cinnamon
1 tbsp. sweet paprika
1/4 tsp. ground ginger
2 tsp. salt
1 tbsp. grated fresh ginger
3 garlic cloves
50 ml lemon juice
100 ml oil

Garnish ingredients
300 ml yogurt
400 g small tomatoes
1 cucumber
2 red onions
1/2 head red cabbage
1 bunch parsley
Juice of 1 lemon

LEG OF LAMB,
PARSLEY SALAD *and*
YOGHURT SAUCE

1. Mix all the ingredients for your spice mix.
2. With a sharp knife, poke 15–20 holes in the leg of lamb and spread the marinade over the leg, making sure to rub it into the holes.
3. Let the leg of lamb to sit in the marinade for at least 1 hour but preferably overnight in the fridge.
4. Heat the oven to 200°C/390°F.
5. Place the leg of lamb in an ovenproof dish. Pour 300 ml of water or stock into the bottom of the dish and roast the leg of lamb for 15 minutes per 0.5 kg. For example, a leg of lamb weighing 1.7 kg must roast for exactly 51 minutes.
6. Once the lamb is cooked, remove from the heat, and let it rest for at least 20 minutes.
7. Cut the red cabbage finely and massage it with fine salt until it is a soft and beautiful purple.
8. Peel the red onion and cut it into thin rings. Marinate it in lemon juice and stir in picked parsley.
9. Cut all greens into suitable sizes for the pita bread.
10. Mix the yogurt and mint and season to taste.
11. Heat the pita and serve immediately.

TIP: *Pack any leftover pitas for lunch/recovery meal the following days. Filled and cold pitas are great for days when you are short of time.*

PITA BREAD

250 ml lukewarm water
2 tsp. dry yeast
1/2 tbsp. maple syrup
395 g wheat flour
+ plus extra for kneading
1 tsp. salt
2 tbsp. olive oil

1. Dissolve the yeast and maple syrup in the water.
2. Add the flour, salt, and olive oil to the mixture and knead into a dough.
3. Let the dough rest, covered, for 10 minutes.
4. Sprinkle a little flour on a clean surface and knead the dough again until it is smooth and flexible. Cover the bowl with plastic film and either leave it in the fridge overnight or let it rest in a warm place for 1 hour until the dough has doubled in size.
5. Heat the oven to 245°C/475°F and place a baking sheet, pizza stone, or cast iron plate on the bottom rack.
6. Fold the dough, divide it into eight equal pieces, and roll each piece into a small ball. Cover the dough-balls with a damp cloth.
7. Roll two dough balls into approx. 3-mm-thick and 20-cm-wide disks. Sprinkle a little flour on them and place them in the oven on the hot plate. Let them bake for approx. 2 minutes or until they puff up. Turn them over and bake them for 1 more minute.
8. Keep the baked pitas warm in a breadbasket covered with a tea towel whilst you finish baking the rest.

TIP: *If you let the dough rest in the fridge overnight to develop the flavor, let it come to room temperature once you take it out of the fridge. Then, knead it and continue from step 5.*

SEARED TUNA
with NECTARINES
Ⓖ Ⓝ Ⓓ **AND LECHE DE TIGRE**

2 red onions

2 nectarines

1 green chili

2 limes

1/2 bunch coriander

400 g fresh tuna
(cut into four 2-cm-thick steaks)

Salt and pepper to taste

Olive oil

1. Peel and cut the onion into thin slices. Grate the lime zest from 1 lime and squeeze the lime juice from both limes over the red onion. Season with a little fine salt.
2. Finely chop the chili. Pick and chop coriander and mix it with the lime juice and onion to make the leche de tigre.
3. Dice the nectarines and mix them with the leche de tigre.
4. Season the tuna steaks with salt and pepper.
5. Heat oil in a pan and fry the tuna steaks for approx. 30–40 seconds on each side. If the steaks are very thick or you would like them more well done, let them cook a little longer; however, tuna steaks are, in my opinion, the tastiest if they have a raw core. Let the steaks rest for 1 minute.
6. Cut the tuna steaks into slices and arrange them beautifully on your favorite plate. Top with the nectarine and leche de tigre.

TIP: *Leche de tigre is a brilliant marinade useful for all types of raw fish. Cut the fish in cubes and let it marinate in the marinade, and you have a fantastic ceviche.*

PLANT-BASED BOLOGNESE

(D) (N) (V)

3 carrots
3 celery stalks
2 onions
2 garlic cloves
250 g red lentils
1 tbsp. dried oregano
1 tbsp. dried basil
1 tsp. dried thyme
4 bay leaves
250 ml red wine (optional but adds flavor)
140 g tomato paste
2 cans peeled tomatoes
150 ml broth
(or water and 1/2 of a stock cube)
Salt and pepper to taste
4 tbsp. olive oil
Balsamic vinegar to taste

1. Peel the carrots, clean the celery, and peel the onion and garlic.
2. Chop the vegetables in a food processor or grate the carrots and finely chop the onion, garlic, and celery by hand.
3. Heat the olive oil in a large heavy-bottomed pan and sauté the vegetables with the dried herbs until completely tender and cooked through. Season with salt and pepper.
4. Add the lentils and heat through.
5. Add the wine (optional) and cook until the liquid is almost completely gone.
6. Add the tomato paste and cook for 2–3 minutes.
7. Add the peeled tomatoes and broth (if you use passata tomatoes, you do not need to add stock). Season with salt and pepper.
8. Bring the mixture to a boil and then turn down the heat to a simmer. Let the dish simmer for approx. 15 minutes.
9. Taste the sauce and season if needed. Serve with freshly cooked pasta, and top with grated cheese and fresh basil.

TIP: *Add fresh rosemary or star anise to make it extra delicious. Make a plant based lasagna with this sauce – it's delicious.*

Easy

 4 people

 60-90 minutes

Peanut CHICKEN

(G) (D)

4 whole bone-in chicken thighs
2 onions
2 garlic cloves
50 g fresh ginger
1 tsp. ground coriander
1 heaping tbsp. peanut butter
1 tin peeled tomatoes (400 g)
1 tbsp. tomato paste
2 star anise
600 g butternut squash
500 ml stock or broth
3 tbsp. olive oil
20 g roasted peanuts
Salt and pepper to taste
Juice and zest of 1 lime

1. Preheat the oven to 175°C/345°F.
2. Split the chicken thighs at the joint to separate the upper and lower thighs.
3. Season the thighs with salt and pepper on both sides and brown the chicken skin in 1 tbsp. olive oil in a large braising pan or regular pan over medium-high heat. Remove the chicken from the pan.
4. Slice the onion and garlic, grate the ginger, and roughly dice the butternut squash.
5. Add 2 tbsp. oil to the pan and caramelize the onion, garlic, and ginger over medium heat together with the star anise and coriander until golden brown. Make sure that all the delicious fond (the brown bits stuck to the pan) from the chicken at the bottom of the pan are scraped up and mixed with the onions.
6. Add the butternut squash.
7. Place the chicken in the pan tugged between the vegetables and add the stock, peeled tomatoes, and tomato paste. Season with salt and pepper.
8. Cover the pan with a lid or foil and cook the dish approx. 25 minutes. Remove the lid and cook for a further 25–30 minutes or until the chicken is nice and tender and the vegetables are well cooked.
9. Season the dish with salt, pepper, and lime juice and zest before serving.
10. Serve with rice noodles and chopped peanuts.

12 Medjool dates

200 ml boiling water

1 pinch fine salt

20 g butter or coconut oil

400 g Greek yogurt

5 tbsp. maple syrup

1/2 vanilla pod

4 bananas

25 g rolled oats

1. Preheat the oven to 170°C/340°F.
2. Toss the oats with 2 tbsp. maple syrup and a little salt. Spread it on a baking sheet covered with baking paper and roast in the oven until golden, about 15 minutes.
3. Pit the dates and blend them with boiling water and salt into a light, caramel-like cream. If the dates are very dry, leave them to soak in boiling water for 5–10 minutes before blending them; make sure they are completely covered by the water.
4. Melt the butter and blend it into the date paste a little at a time. Season to taste with salt.
5. Mix the Greek yogurt with the rest of the maple syrup and the vanilla. You can sweeten it more to taste.
6. Peel and slice the bananas.
7. Add 1 tbsp. date caramel to the bottom of a glass and place the toasted oats on top, followed by the banana slices and yogurt. Finish with more date caramel and a slice of banana.

TIP: *Assemble the dessert in a glass or make a larger portion to be placed in a dish. If you add more melted butter to the date puree, it will be more like caramel curd.*

KARIN LAMBRECHTSE

"FOOD IS PASSION AND FUEL."

Karin Lambrechtse is a Dutch sports dietician who has been working as a consultant in velo-sport for several years. She is contracted to Team Jumbo-Visma. She works in a team with two chefs, and her philosophy is crystal clear. Data must go hand in hand with passion and joy. She has a holistic way of thinking when it comes to fueling the riders and keeping them strong and happy. This way of thinking is apparent when she talks about new trends, lessons learned, and modern nutrition for top riders.

"We always talk about food, I ask the riders what they like, and maybe there are family recipes that they really enjoy. I won't be able to cook their food as well as grandma did. We use a food coach app, and sometimes the riders look on the app to see what they will be eating later on. And it motivates them to work even harder. Sometimes they say, 'Karin, I saw this on the menu, so I'll push even harder.' So they know they can eat more. I try to listen to them. It is a collaboration. I think it's important that we remember that we're dealing with a human and not a machine. I believe their nutrition is part of their physical and mental recovery from the moment they arrive at the table after a stage. So yes, holistic in that sense."

Given her background, it makes sense that she works with food in a way that combines performance and passion. The mind must be happy for the body to perform at its best when needed.

"My background has nothing to do with cycling. It is both ballet and dance. I was a dancer for 11 years, which is a tough sport. But as a dancer, you don't really think about it. You're more like an artist, and you don't see yourself as an athlete. But nutrition was interesting for me, I grew up in the north of Holland, and my dad grew vegetables in the garden. I was always playing outside, and I always enjoyed the pure taste of food. As a dancer, I had to take care of myself and my body. You must be thin but still perform at an intense level."

This understanding of food and sport turned into a philosophy of food and performance, she says.

THERE ARE FIVE CORNERSTONES TO UNDER-STANDING NUTRITION.

- "The first one is knowledge. Do research and dive into nutrition. What are carbs, and what are proteins? How does it work? How has it been digested? And how does it work for you? What is your background? If you're from Japan, you're not going to eat oats. You may want to eat rice, so improve your knowledge somehow."

- "And then the second one is quality. What is the quality of the food I eat? Is it fresh? Is it in season? Is it frozen or canned?"

- "The third one is quantity. If you know the quantity you want and if you have the knowledge, how much do you need of that product? It's always important to know your needs. If you have a long training day or a heavy training day, you have to eat more than when you're on a rest day. But sometimes, when you have a heavy day, it's hard to eat much. So, be smart and eat extra food in the evening before a heavy day, as well as extra food the next day. "

- "Timing is number four. If you eat the right things at the right time, it is going to be much more beneficial. Protein is not used up if you eat it right before exercising. Timing is essential when it comes to sports."

- "And then the fifth thing is planning and preparation. What is my week going to look like? When are my heavy training sessions? When are my free days? Planning is winning."

Being a modern chef and cooking for riders entails more than just knowing how to cook pasta and wield a large knife. Karen Lambrechtse uses a food coach app, among other tools, to stay on top of what the riders need for the next day's stage. This app keeps her and the riders up to date with what they always need. She prepares the food, and the app tells the individual riders what to eat at specific times.

"The app is connected to a Garmin that they use. Their coach plans the training in the back end of the app. The rider then loads their home training. The app syncs the data, and it adjusts automatically, stating what they should eat. Some have families, so it adjusts the number of people enjoying the meal. They can also put their own recipes in the app, and they can use it at home."

Karin Lambrechtse and her team start planning for the Tour de France months ahead of time, and various camps provide valuable information. The altitude camps provide her with valuable information about the riders' nutritional needs.

"Some riders are specialists at riding at high altitudes. We call them the mountain goats at the altitude camp. We camp there for three to four weeks, depending on whether they have to race or not. Usually, there are two altitude stages or training camps. For example, after the Dauphiné, there is a one-and-a-half-week altitude camp before the tour. We try to get them there as much as possible so the body can adjust."

"They eat low-fiber food all day, usually for two days before a mountain stage, to lose a little weight because you don't need all of the fiber stuck in your intestinal tract. They lose 500g to 1.5kg, without losing strength. We also try to communicate with the riders, because sometimes they feel really empty. Their muscle glycogen is restored and replenished, but it doesn't feel like that because they're not feeling full. Therefore, we test specific kinds of meals in the altitude stages or at training camps. They must get used to this feeling that their body and muscle glycogen are full, but they don't feel full. It is an important lesson."

Food and diets must not be a strict, boring regime, she says. What works 100 percent for one rider might only work 75 percent for another rider. Chefs will learn, and so will the riders.

"If a rider thinks something is good for them, we evaluate it at home. They can train with no carbs and see how they feel. If I tell them they cannot do it, they will do it anyway. So, it's better to keep in touch, keep an eye on what they are doing, and talk about lessons learned."

According to Karin, the riders' energy use in an hour is equivalent to one regular meal. What they are eating on the bike is just keeping fuel in the tank.

Karin Lambrechtse says she is always looking for ways to optimize nutrition programs. Can things be done faster, in another way, or more efficiently? The combination of a specific diet strategy and location must keep the riders happy and increase their team spirit.

"Between Dauphiné and the tour, the families of the riders can come, and we cook for them as well because some have young babies. It's a kind of special service that we have. They can either stay at our house, or grab and go, or we can deliver food to wherever they are staying. So yeah, I think it's a good way for them to focus on the big races. We also have an altitude camp in Tenerife for the Giro. And then we have one in the Sierra for the Tour and the Vuelta. So, it's changing in the Alps. But all the big races have two camps for preparation."

Test results are used to plan menus and diets. When the big races are on, the riders can check the app to see what's on the menu. There are no surprises; all the recipes are tested and known to the riders.

"We test recipes on altitude stages, or training camps, so they can give their feedback. All the meals that they eat are familiar to them. Nothing new is suddenly sprung upon them."

The Tour de France is a busy time for the team of chefs.

"Usually, the day before the race is a carb-loading day. And then on rest days, it's more carb-focused, but not necessarily carb-loading. We don't do three or four days of carb loading. It is just one day before the start of the race."

When the race is on, the preparation of food is another kind of marathon to make sure every rider is fueled up and ready to go. The chefs are busy preparing and cooking food, and for some chefs and teams, it can be a logistical challenge as well. If the team's food truck is without an oven, or equipped for service but not cooking food, then they must use hotel kitchens if possible.

"Breakfast is oats or rice porridge depending on the stage. If it's a really heavy stage, then we serve rice porridge. If not, it's oats or pancakes. We have French toast and low-fat croissants as well on rest days, stuff that offers some variation. But this depends on the group. Some of them just prefer the basics, and that's enough. However, we frequently have some guys in the tour group who have very refined tastes. So, they are happy when there's something different every day. It may be normal oats, or double chocolate oats, or banana oats. But besides oats, it's fruit and toast. We also have cappuccinos on the menu because it's a kind of ritual for them."

"They must have good coffee. I don't know if it was the same back then, but now we always carry this big coffee machine."

Then there are snacks and refuels for the during and after stage meals. Karin tells new riders who join the team to eat more when the race is on than they normally do. Otherwise, it will catch up on you later in the race, but don't overeat she says. You don't want to feel heavy.

After the race, it's time for mathematics and calculations in order to get the riders' energy back on track. The post-race meals and snacks are important, and then it is dinner time.

"It's the same meal for everyone, but they have their individual portion sizes because we sometimes have to adjust what they eat. Whether they had a heavier stage or maybe a less heavy stage, we must adjust the quantities. For example, the chicken cannot be inside the pasta, so it's separated. But we don't want to make it look dull. There needs to be some color, and usually, we have two or three carb components, such as bread, pasta, and some other form of carbs. This can be gnocchi, or noodles, or naan bread, or something other than pasta or rice. We must have a protein source that can be any protein. But when the protein sources are small, we may make chicken burgers, and we put rice puffs or some other carbs inside the burgers."

When it comes to dinner and evening snacks, Karin and the rest of the team keep a close eye on the intake of fat. Olive oil is kept to a minimum for cooking, and this is not because the chefs are scared of fat.

"The amount of fat we use is low. At dinner, the olive oil is separate from all the other components that they can put on their plates. So, before we cook, we measure the olive oil that we can use in the kitchen, and we try to use as little as possible so they can add some to their food at the table. The table is well stocked with ketchup, chutney, olive oil, and other condiments. The less we use in the kitchen, the more they can use."

The future will likely see more tools like apps and AI determining the nutrition profile of the riders. Asked how she sees the future of nutrition for the riders, she says:

"I also asked my team to think about where nutrition coaching may be in 10 years. They came up with all sorts of ideas, like scanning blood to see in a microsample what must be replenished. Or you may have food printers. But I think where we are now is enough. I don't know if we need to go any further with AI. It's great to use it to calculate stuff because it will be impossible to do that for 28 riders. But for me, the fun part is being creative with the numbers. So, I can decide that the carb can be potato, or it can be rice, and then I can still be creative with those components. I think food should be prepared with passion. Food for humans made by humans."

Words from a true artist!

STAGE

Difficult

 24 pieces

 90 minutes

GYOZA with MANDELRUSHROOMS

(D) (N) (V) *with* **MUSHROOMS**

240 g wheat flour

120 ml boiling water
(straight from the kettle or pot)

1/2 tsp. salt

3 carrots

200 g mushrooms of your choice

3 garlic cloves

2 tbsp. + 1 tsp. olive oil

1/4 bunch chopped fresh coriander

Salt to taste

1/2 tbsp. soy sauce

1 tbsp. rice wine or white wine vinegar

2 tsp. toasted sesame oil

1 tsp. chili oil or a sprinkle of dried chili

TIP: *You can add minced meat to the filling. Prep as many as you can and freeze them for later.*

1. Sift the flour into a bowl and dissolve the salt in the boiling water.
2. Add the water a little at a time to the flour and gradually make a dough. Knead the dough by hand (or via a mixer with a hook) for 10 minutes.
3. Divide the dough into two equal-size parts and roll them into two balls. Wrap each roll firmly in plastic wrap and let the rolls rest in the fridge for at least 30 minutes. Meanwhile, make the filling.
4. Clean all greens.
5. Chop the carrots and garlic in a mini chopper; then, chop the mushrooms separately. You can also use a grater or slicer.
6. Heat 2 tbsp. olive oil in a pan and sauté the carrots, garlic, and mushrooms for 6–7 minutes. Season with salt and fresh coriander. Let the filling cool while you roll the gyoza skins.
7. Divide each roll of dough into small pieces and roll each piece into a ball. Make sure the dough always stays moist by keeping it covered with a damp tea towel.
8. Flatten the balls one at a time and roll them out very thinly, approx. 1/2 mm thick. Cut out a perfect circle of dough with a metal dough cutter or glass.
9. Stack the gyoza skins, sprinkling flour between each piece. Remember to keep them covered with a damp cloth.
10. Place a gyoza skin on a cutting board. Place a teaspoon of filling in the middle and brush one half of the skin at the edge with water.
11. Close the gyoza by folding the edges of the dough together, making small overlaps along the folded side.
12. When all the gyoza skins are folded, place them in a cold non-stick pan with 1 tsp. sesame oil and 1/2 dl water.
13. Cover the pan with the lid, turn the heat to medium-high, and let the gyoza steam up and become crispy on the bottom.
14. Mix the soy sauce, vinegar, sesame oil, and chili oil together and serve the sauce in small bowls.
15. Immediately serve the freshly fried gyoza with the dipping sauce.

Easy

 4 people

 30 minutes

ROASTED FENNEL
(G) (D) (V) *with* CITRUS AND PISTACHIO

2 fennel bulbs
1 orange
1 pink grapefruit
2 small red onions
25 g pistachios
2 tbsp. maple syrup or honey
Juice and zest of 2 limes
1/2 bunch dill
1/2 tsp. salt
Salt and pepper to taste
2 tbsp. neutral cooking oil

1. Rinse all the greens and peel the onion.
2. Cut off the top and bottom of the orange and grapefruit and Cut the peel off with a sharp knife.
3. Slice the orange and grapefruit crosswise and then chop the pistachios.
4. Cut a thin slice off the bottom of the fennel bulbs to clean them. Then half the bulbs lengthwise and cut one and a half bulb into wedges. Slice the last half thinly on a mandolin slicer.
5. Cut the onions into thin rings, preferably using a mandolin slicer. Toss the onion rings together with the maple syrup and the lime juice and finely grated zest. Season with salt and pepper and let it marinade while the fennel is being fried.
6. Heat 1 tbsp. oil in a pan and fry the fennel wedges for approx. 2–3 minutes on each side over medium-high heat so that they color nicely on both cut surfaces. The wedges must be tender.
7. Arrange the fennel wedges, sliced fennel, orange, and grapefruit beautifully on a plate. Top with the pickled red onions, fresh dill, and pistachio.

Easy

 2-4 people

 10-15 minutes

FRIED RICE

Ⓖ Ⓓ Ⓥ WITH *bulgogi sauce*

Bulgogi sauce

50 ml soy sauce

1 tsp. toasted sesame oil

2 tbsp. maple syrup

1/2 tsp. black pepper

1 tsp. grated ginger

1 clove grated garlic

Fried rice

400 g cooked rice

3 eggs

2 red onions

250 g broccoli

200 g edamame beans

2 tbsp. olive oil

Salt to taste

1. Mix all sauce ingredients in a bowl and set aside.
2. Finely slice the onions and broccoli.
3. Heat 1 tbsp. olive oil in a pan and fry the rice until it is very hot.
4. Add the onions and fry for 1 minute over medium-high heat.
5. Add the rest of the vegetables and cook until all vegetables are tender.
6. Season to taste with salt.
7. Make a hole in the middle of the rice and pour 1 tbsp. oil on the pan. Crack the eggs into the hole and scramble them until almost cooked. Then, stir the eggs into the rice mixture until well mixed.
8. Season the dish with salt and serve topped with bulgogi sauce.

TIP: *You can cook large amounts of rice and freeze it in portions for later use, such as when you need to cook quickly. You can use all kinds of vegetables for a dish like this. Feel free to add fresh coriander or mint.*
Bring the bulgogi sauce to a boil and reduce it to a thicker consistency.

Easy

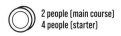 2 people (main course)
4 people (starter)

 30 minutes

SALMON FOIL PACKS *with*
HERBS AND WHITE WINE

(G) (D) (N)

4 pieces salmon (approx. 80-100 g each)
4 tbsp. maple syrup
4 tbsp. white wine vinegar
1 tbsp. yellow mustard seeds
1/4 pointed cabbage
1 zucchini
1/4 bunch dill
200 ml white wine
1 tbsp. butter
Salt and pepper to taste

1. Preheat the oven to 180°C/355°F.
2. Heat the vinegar and maple syrup with the mustard seeds and let them steep for 10 minutes.
3. Finely slice the zucchini and pointed cabbage.
4. Place two pieces of foil on a flat surface and place a slightly smaller piece of baking paper on top. The foil must be large enough to wrap loosely around the fish.
5. Place the sliced greens at the bottom and the salmon on top of each piece of baking paper and season with salt and pepper.
6. Fold up the sides of the foil to make small bowls and pour white wine into them. Place a spoonful of mustard seed marinade over each salmon and top with 1/2 tbsp. butter.
7. Close up the foil bowls. Make sure steam can circulate around inside.
8. Bake for approx. 10–15 minutes or until a skewer slides effortlessly through the fish.
9. Top the fish with fresh dill and serve with rice, potatoes, or fresh pasta on the side.

TIP: *This dish makes fantastic leftovers for lunch the following day, served cold in a salad or as a filling in a sandwich or wrap.*

Easy

 2-4 people

 20 minutes

Pink GINGER RICE
(G) (D) (N)
WITH SASHIMI SALMON

200 g sashimi salmon
1 beetroot
Fresh ginger
50 ml white wine vinegar
50 ml mirin or maple syrup
50 ml soy sauce
1/2 pointed cabbage
3 scallions
1 courgette
400 g cooked brown rice
1 cucumber
100 g sugar snap peas
1 sheet nori seaweed
1 tbsp. sesame seeds

1. Cut the salmon into thin slices and keep it in the fridge while the rest of the ingredients are being prepared.
2. Peel the beetroot and ginger and grate it very finely.
3. Cut the pointed cabbage finely, slice the scallions and julienne the courgette into matchstick shapes.
4. Cut the cucumber and sugar snap peas into thin strips.
5. Mix the vinegar, mirin, and soy sauce with the beetroot, ginger, rice, courgette, and scallions.
6. Arrange the rice mixture in a bowl and top with the salmon and nori seaweed. Place the cucumber and sugar snap peas on the side and sprinkle sesame seeds over the dish.

IMPORTANT: *Make sure the fish is suitable for being eaten raw; ask your local fishmonger.*

Easy

 20 minutes

◯ 4 people

GREEN ASPARAGUS *with*

Ⓖ Ⓝ Ⓥ **CILANTRO SAUCE**

4 eggs
1 bunch green asparagus
1 large bunch coriander
1 garlic clove
1 small green chili (optional)
Juice and zest of 1 lime
200 ml Greek yogurt
1 tbsp. olive oil
Salt and pepper to taste

1. Bring enough water to cover the eggs to a boil in a saucepan. Boil the eggs for 6–7 minutes. Cool in cold water immediately. Use the egg guide at the back of the book to determine the cooking time of the eggs.
2. Rinse the green asparagus and break off the hard part at the bottom.
3. Rinse and pick the coriander. If the stems are soft and fresh, you can chop them finely.
4. Peel the garlic and chop the chili (adjusting the amount according to how spicy you want the coriander crème).
5. Blend the yogurt, coriander, grated garlic, and chili with a stick blender. Add lime zest and juice, salt, and pepper to taste.
6. Heat up the olive oil in a pan, sprinkle with a little fine salt, and fry the asparagus over high heat for 1 minute or until cooked but still nicely green.
7. Peel and halve the eggs.
8. Arrange the asparagus on top of the coriander crème on a plate and top with egg.

TIP: *You can serve any spring vegetable with this sauce.*

GYODON
- RICE *with* MINCED BEEF AND FRIED EGG

3 onions
2 garlic cloves
1 knob fresh ginger
1/2 bunch spring onions
2 carrots
200 g mushrooms
400 g minced beef
100 ml soy sauce
50 ml mirin or maple syrup
400 g rice
Toasted sesame seeds
4 eggs
Salt
1-2 tbsp. olive oil

1. Peel and mince the onion and garlic and then clean and finely grate the ginger.
2. Peel the carrots and grate them roughly. Cut the mushrooms into thin slices.
3. Heat 1–2 tbsp. oil in a pan and brown the meat well over medium-high heat. Make sure to spread it well during frying so that you don't have large lumps of mince clumping together.
4. Add the onion, garlic, carrot, mushrooms, and ginger and sauté until tender over medium heat, approx. 5–6 minutes.
5. Cook the rice according to the instructions on the bag.
6. Add the soy sauce and mirin or maple syrup to the meat together with 50 ml of water and let reduce to half over low heat whilst stirring. Season with salt.
7. Fry the eggs.
8. Serve the rice in bowls topped with the beef and fried egg (one per bowl).

TIP: *Serve this dish with the only vegetables as in the recipe, or with baked fish or roasted chicken instead of beef.*

Easy

 30 servings

 5 minutter

FURIKAKE SPRINKLES

(G) (D) (N) (V)

50 g white sesame seeds
50 g black sesame seeds
1 tbsp. fine salt
1 tbsp. sugar
4 sheets nori seaweed

Optional: Bonito flakes,
Dried chili powder, Kelp,
Shiitake powder

1. Grind the white sesame seeds in a mini chopper or with a pestle and mortar to a coarse consistency. Cut the nori seaweed into small pieces and grind it into a sprinkle texture, if necessary, using a mini chopper.
2. Toast the chopped white sesame seeds in a pan over medium heat until golden brown.
3. Mix the toasted sesame seeds, black sesame seeds, seaweed, sugar, and salt together.
4. Store in an airtight container at room temperature.

TIP: *Add 1/2 tsp. chili powder to the mixture if you want it to be spicy. Serve with fish, chicken, or vegetable dishes or as a side dish with rice dishes.*

RICK ZABEL

Pro rider since 2012

Rick Zabel grew up watching his father Erik race and win at extremely high speeds. As a teenager, Rick Zabel became a rider himself. For more than ten years as a pro, he had first-hand experience of how good nutrition not only changed the food on the plate but also changed the sport.

"I was born in a small town called Unna. It is close to Dortmund. And I guess it's famous because it's home to Borussia Dortmund, a well-known football club. My father was a professional as well. So, I grew up watching him win big races as a professional cyclist. And I always liked the sport, but I never really saw myself as a professional rider. I played soccer instead. I stopped playing soccer when I was 12 or 13 years old, and I didn't do any sport for a year or two. My parents asked me if I wanted to try cycling because I always liked to ride my bike. It was when I was 14 or 15 that I started to win my first races."

In his early years, nutrition was not really a thing to be considered. He remembers that it was more important to eat a big breakfast and ride it out.

"My dad is a little old school. With all the nutrition facts we know now, you could say maybe he did everything wrong. I grew up hearing him say that you should eat as much as you can for breakfast. And then for the first two to three hours on the bike, you don't eat anything because you're so full from breakfast. Maybe you have one or two energy bars with you, and that's it."

"I remember hearing that drinking is a sign of weakness and stuff like that. Now I consider this very unhealthy. I remember training camps in Mallorca where I would book a hotel with only breakfast and dinner. So, when I came home from a training ride, I would eat a small bowl of cereal or something similar. And then I would starve until dinnertime and eat as much as possible to fuel up for the next day. Nowadays, we know how to do it better."

Some riders see food as a necessary evil and focus mainly on the long training hours. Rick Zabel will not have one without the other.

"I would say training and nutrition are very important partners. These two elements should be planned together. Things have changed a lot in the last ten years. My father and I believed in the early days that it was more about being skinny. To be skinny, you had to eat as little as possible. That was all we heard. And then, every year, you would see how the nutrition information became more scientific. Nowadays, every team has a nutritionist, and you get all the stuff that you need, from vitamins and minerals like magnesium to probiotics. Now we have cooks at our races and at our training camps, where we have two chefs who serve us lunch, dinner, and breakfast every day. It's easier for us riders because we can basically just go there and take whatever we want because it's only good healthy stuff. I think the nutrition part is the biggest game changer of the last few years because just knowing when, where, and what to eat makes such a big difference. If you had asked me about this five or 10 years ago, I would have known nothing."

Rick Zabel prefers not to be too strict about his diet and eating habits, but some planning is necessary, he says, depending on your goals for the season.

"It depends on the time of the year and on the riders. I would say that for the climbers and the guys who need to watch their weight, eating must be stricter than for someone like me. But if your goal is the Tour de France, then your team must start preparing in December and January. At team camps, we track our weight and fat percentages, and our goal is to be ready for the Tour de France in July. We try to be as healthy as possible for the race."

"We also get daily plans when the nutritionist looks at our performance, but generally, the coaches design the training programs. The nutritionist will do research and give us a plan, explaining how to eat during the next week."

"Of course, it's mentally challenging when you look at how many carbs, proteins, and other stuff you need to eat every day. So, for me, it's also important when the important race is over. Then the team leaves you alone for a while, and you can just eat what you want."

Off-season and at home, Rick Zabel prefers an easy start to the day.

"I take my son to kindergarten at eight o'clock in the morning. And luckily, it's just 20 minutes away from where we live. I have breakfast with my wife when I get back home."

"A typical breakfast begins with a cappuccino for both of us, followed by some cereal with yogurt and fruit like bananas and strawberries, or blue-berries. We add Greek yogurt as a topping."

"This is maybe 30% of my breakfasts, and for the other 70%, I eat German bread. I love German bread, and I eat it with cheese or ham. It depends on how hungry I am, but it's at least four or five slices of bread with cheese, marmalade, or cold cuts. Then I go out for a ride."

> *"I do not weigh my food. I just eat and enjoy the mornings with my wife."*

These mornings are very different from those during cycling season, especially during the Tour de France.

"Yeah, for sure, it's very different. The number of calories we must eat is way more. I would say it starts already with the schedule we get the day before a race. So, normally, we have breakfast three hours before the race starts in order to have enough time to digest everything. A normal stage lasts four to five hours. So, I eat a large portion of porridge, adding maple syrup and a banana or some berries. And most of the time, we get pancakes to cheer us up. I like to eat pancakes with peanut butter and honey. I eat two or three pancakes and one or two slices of bread. This is a big breakfast, for sure. We may also have an omelet, but I don't eat an omelet every day. I usually order an omelet every second day. Before the start of a stage, there is a little buffet in the bus with a variety of gels, energy bars, and rice cakes laid out for us."

During a stage, Rick Zabel does not need to feel full, but he maintains a steady intake to keep his energy levels up.

"I always try to take in at least 80 grams of carbs per hour. I know if I do that, I'll feel fine and won't suffer from low energy levels or hunger. Then, when I finish the race, I eat again as fast as possible."

"Normally, there is a rice cooker on the bus, and everyone eats a bowl of rice mixed with some tuna, or we add different sauces for flavor. This is straight after a race, and we are told what to eat after a race. It is important to fuel up again as fast as possible after a race and then have another snack two hours later."

"At the hotel, we have a massage, and then it's time for dinner again. It's normal to first eat a lar-ge portion of rice or pasta, whatever you prefer. I'm more of a pasta guy. I like pasta. We have a chef, so we get a variety of pasta dishes every day. Some guys like plain pasta, which they just put oil and cheese on, but normally our cook prepares carbonara or pasta with tomato sauce. As our chefs buy fresh products, we are asked the day before if we want a steak for dinner or something else. Salmon and chicken are always on the menu."

Some teams or individual riders weigh their food to keep track of their intake and calculate if they need more of one thing or another. Rick Zabel prefers not to do that. Why not?

"Because for me, that's too much. I do not like it. Most riders do it, but not with chicken or steak. They don't weigh the meat, but they do weigh the pasta and rice. Of course, if you do the general classification, it's necessary. The race is extremely hard, and you race every day for two weeks. So, there is no chance you will gain weight; you can never eat too much. For me, it's a problem if I don't eat enough, and I'm not good the next day because my body is empty. For me, it is not about eating a minimum it is about eating enough."

Rick Zabel prefers to be in control of his intake, but he does take advice from the team's nutritionist.

"We have one full-time nutritionist, and he will cover all the training camps and the biggest races. He will be at the Tour de France, but he cannot be at every race. Sometimes there are different races at the same time. Some riders like me don't really need his help every day, but other riders like to have daily contact with him. The nutritionist always looks at the next race's details. Is it one week? How many time trials, and how many stages are there? He prepares a general eating plan for the riders, detailing what to eat and how many calories and carbs to consume. He gives a helpful guideline."

Rick Zabel's advice to a hopeful young rider would be to gain knowledge and enjoy the sport.

"Yes, my main advice would be to gain knowledge, especially on how to fuel your body when on the bike, because this is the most important part."

"You must understand how much carbohydrate your body can tolerate. The carbohydrates fuel your body on the bike. They give you power. So, it is very important to know the correct carbohydrate intake for your body. It's as important as being strict with yourself. It's okay to let loose sometimes and not be strict all the time. It is very important for me to be mentally happy and enjoy my food."

Green SUMMER SALAD
Ⓖ Ⓝ Ⓥ WITH POTATOES

500 g boiled new potatoes
100 g fresh parsley (a bunch of parsley)
20 g fresh chives (1/2 bunch)
2-3 radishes
1/2 cucumber
100 ml mild olive oil
2 tbsp. apple cider vinegar + extra to taste
1 tsp. salt
2 ml Greek yogurt
1 tbsp. Dijon mustard
2 tbsp. smoked fresh cheese
2 pieces dark rye bread/pumpernickel

1. Chop or blend the rye bread into crumbs.
2. Heat a pan to medium-high heat with 2 tbsp. oil and add the breadcrumbs. Toast the crumbs in the pan at medium heat, whilst stirring until completely crispy.
3. Rinse the herbs and spin or shake dry.
4. Pick the parsley off the stems and chop roughly. Cut chives into 3-cm sticks. Pour boiling water over the herbs, leave for a few seconds, and then squeeze all water off.
5. Chop the blanched herbs and then blend them with Dijon mustard, vinegar, honey, and salt into a smooth, beautiful green puree.
6. Blend in the oil little by little.
7. Stir the yogurt and smoked fresh cheese together with the herb puree and season with salt and apple cider vinegar.
8. Fold the potatoes into the herb cream and arrange the potato salad with radishes and cucumber on a pretty plate. Top with crispy rye breadcrumbs and serve for a happy summer's day.

TIP: *If you can't get smoked fresh cheese, like the one I use in Denmark, you can use any type of low fat fresh cheese and then just season it with smoked salt.*

Medium

 4 people

 50 minutes

FLANK STEAK
WITH *baked* TOMATOES AND CHIMICHURRI

300 g small tomatoes
1 bunch parsley or fresh coriander
2 tbsp. capers
1 small shallot
1 small garlic clove
1 tbsp. red wine vinegar
4 tbsp. olive oil
1 tbsp. honey
1 tbsp. balsamic vinegar
600 g flank steak
Salt and pepper to taste

1. Preheat the oven to 165°C/330°F.
2. Rinse the tomatoes and poke small holes in them with a knife.
3. Toss the tomatoes with balsamic vinegar, honey, and 1 tbsp. of olive oil and season with salt and pepper. Then, place them on a small baking tray lined with baking paper.
4. Bake the tomatoes for approx. 30 minutes.
5. To make the herby sauce, chimichurri, first rinse, pick and chop the parsley.
6. Coarsely chop the capers, finely mince the shallot, and mix them with the vinegar in a bowl.
7. Pat the steak dry with a paper towel and season with salt and pepper.
8. Heat 1 tbsp. oil in a pan over high heat. Place the steak in the pan and brown it nicely. Turn the heat down slightly and cook the meat for 4–5 minutes on each side over medium-high heat. Then, remove from the heat. If you want your flank steak well-done or if it's thicker than 4cm/1,5 inches, your cooking time will be longer.
9. Let the meat rest while you mix 2 tbsp. olive oil with the vinegar–onion mixture. Season to taste with salt and pepper.
10. Cut the steak and serve it with the baked tomatoes and chimichurri and a side dish, such as potato salad.

TIP: *Always let the meat rest after cooking before cutting it.*

Easy

 12 servings

 60 minutes

LEMON CAKE *with*

(G) (N) (V) **CHEESE FROSTING**

Cake:

275 g sweet potato
3 eggs
150 g honey or maple syrup
90 g millet flakes
30 g rice flour
1 lemon
1 vanilla pod, seeds scraped out
1 tsp. baking powder
1/2 tsp. salt

Frosting:

200 g cottage cheese
100 g Greek yogurt
Juice of 1 lemon
2 tbsp. maple syrup
1 pinch salt

1. Preheat the oven to 170°C.
2. Peel the sweet potato and dice it.
3. Blend all cake ingredients in the food processor using the pulse function until the mixture reaches a mazarine-like consistency. Keep an eye on it, as the batter can get very watery if you blend it for too long. If you don't have a food processor, you will have to grate the sweet potato and then mix all ingredients together in a bowl; blend it with a stick blender to make the batter as smooth as possible.
4. Grease a cake tin and dust it with rice flour. Pour in the batter. Level the top of the batter with a wet dough scraper or spoon.
5. Bake it on the center rack for 35–40 minutes or until the cake feels firm, yet spongy. If your cake tin is very large and the cake is very flat, the baking time will be slightly shorter; if the cake tin is very tall, the baking time could be a little longer. Use a cake tester to test whether the cake is ready; if the batter sticks to the needle, it needs a little more time.
6. To make the glaze, first blend the cottage cheese into a smooth puree in a blender or mini chopper.
7. Add the rest of the ingredients to the chopper, blend, and season with more salt and lemon juice to taste.
8. Once the cake has cooled, top with the cheese frosting.

TIP: *You can use rolled oats instead of millet flakes. You can also use cream cheese instead of cottage cheese or simply top the cake with yogurt flavored with lemon and maple syrup.*

REST DAY

Easy

 4 people

 25 minutes

SALAD NIÇOISE

G D N

4 eggs
1 head romaine lettuce
1 small red radicchio
200 g broccolini
200 g small tomatoes
400 g new boiled potatoes
50 g small black olives
1 red onion
2 tbsp. Dijon mustard
2 tbsp. red wine vinegar
1–2 anchovy fillets (optional)
1 small garlic clove
100 ml olive oil
2 cans good-quality tuna
Salt and pepper to taste

1. Bring a pot of water to a boil. Carefully drop the eggs into the boiling water and cook for 8 minutes. Set a timer! Then, cool them immediately in cold water.
2. Rinse all greens.
3. Cut the romaine lettuce and radicchio into 3-cm-wide pieces and halve the tomatoes.
4. Rinse the broccolini and cut off the bottom. Blanch for 10 seconds until tender with some bite and beautifully green. Shock in cold water.
5. Finely mince the red onion.
6. With a stick blender, blend the vinegar, mustard, anchovies, and grated garlic together with the olive oil. Season with salt and pepper to taste.
7. Mix the minced red onions into the dressing and let sit for 10 minutes.
8. Cut the potatoes into bite-size pieces.
9. Peel the eggs and half them.
10. Toss the lettuce, tomato, potatoes and olives together with the dressing and arrange on a pretty plate. Top with tuna and boiled eggs.

TIP: *Use fresh tuna steaks instead of canned tuna. Sear them and slice them.*

Easy 1 bread

 2 days + 60 minutes

(D) (N) (V) **DUTCH OVEN BREAD**

400 ml water
5 g active yeast or 1.5 g dry yeast
150 g whole wheat flour
350 g all-purpose wheat flour
7.5 g fine salt
50-75 g sourdough (if you have any)

TIP: You can also make bread rolls from this dough. Divide the dough with a dough spatula into 10–12 pieces. Roll the pieces in kernels, seeds, or flour and place them on baking paper to rise. The baking time will be shortened to approx. 12–14 minutes. Use the trick beneath to bake bread rolls.

Dough:

1. Dissolve the yeast and sourdough in lukewarm water and stir in the flour until combined.
2. Add the salt and knead the dough for at least 5 minutes, preferably in a mixer, until the dough feels firm and springy.
3. Remove the dough hook from the mixer, cover the bowl, and let the dough rise for 1 hour at room temperature.
4. Fold the dough over itself 6–8 times until it is firm again and turn it upside down in the bowl. Cover the bowl and let the dough rise for 1–2 days in the fridge. Check it regularly so that it doesn't swell. Fold the dough as described twice a day.
5. Take the dough out of the fridge and allow it to reach room temperature.
6. Fold the dough like a small envelope by folding the sides in and then folding the bottom part up and the top part down so that you "close" the envelope.
7. Roll the dough in flour and let it rise on a large piece of baking paper or in a breadbasket or bread mold until it doubles in size.

Baking:

1. Preheat the oven to 220°C/430°F.
2. Heat a cast iron dutch oven/pot on a rack in the middle of the oven.
3. Turn the bread out onto baking paper and make a cut on the top with a sharp knife or bread knife.
4. Transfer the baking paper and bread dough into the dutch oven/pot.
5. Place the dutch oven/pot on a rack in the middle of the oven and pour 100 ml of boiling water into the bottom of the pot underneath the baking paper and quickly put the lid on.
6. Bake for approx. 30 minutes or until the bread risen and open up nicely. Remove the lid and finish baking the bread until it is nicely toasted and dark brown. The Bread should sound hollow when tapped on the bottom.
7. Leave to cool on a wire rack before slicing.

Easy

 2 people

 15 minutes

CARBONARA WITH CHERVIL and ASPARAGUS

1 bunch asparagus
2 red onions
1 small garlic clove
1 bunch chervil (French parsley)
2 eggs
25 g parmesan or pecorino
1 tbsp. olive oil
200 g spaghetti
Salt to taste

1. Bring a pot of salted water to a boil.
2. Clean the asparagus and peel the onion and garlic. Rinse the chervil and chop it coarsely.
3. Cut the asparagus into bite-size pieces, finely chop the onion, and finely grate the garlic.
4. Blend the eggs and chervil with an immersion blender.
5. Grate the parmesan or pecorino.
6. Cook the pasta.
7. When there are 3 minutes left of the pasta cooking time, heat up the olive oil in a sauté pan and sauté the onion and garlic over medium heat. Season with salt.
8. Add the asparagus and let it cook for 1–2 minutes. They must be beautifully green and have a bite.
9. Once the pasta is cooked, transfer it to the pan with the onion and asparagus; a little pasta water is welcome to moisten things up a bit. Mix it all together.
10. Add the egg mixture and remove the pan from the heat. Stir while the egg mixture thickens, but do not allow the eggs to become scrambled.
11. Add the grated cheese and stir until nice and creamy. Season with salt and pepper and serve immediately.

TIP: *You can use any kind of fresh herbs or greens, such as peas or spinach.*

Easy

 4-6 people

 60 minutes

BAKED BEETROOT *and*

Ⓖ Ⓥ TZATZIKI SALAD

600 g beetroots
25 g pine nuts
2 cucumbers
3 tbsp. Greek yogurt
1/2 garlic clove
1 bunch dill
Juice and zest of 1 lemon
1 tbsp. olive oil
Salt and pepper to taste

1. Preheat the oven to 200°C.
2. Place the beetroots in pairs on a double layer of foil, drizzle with olive oil, and season with salt. Wrap the foil tightly around the beetroots and bake for 45–50 minutes or until completely tender. (The baking time will change depending on the size of the beetroots. Large beets may need more time and to be wrapped in the foil individually, whereas small beets will cook faster.) Once cooked, open the foil and let the beetroots cool and then rub off the skin..
3. Toast the pine nuts on a dry pan over low-medium heat. REMEMBER: They'll burn the second you take your eyes off them! Season with salt.
4. Peel the cucumbers, cut them into quarters lengthwise, and cut out the seeds. Cut into small cubes and season with salt.
5. Chop 2/3 of the dill.
6. Mix the yogurt with minced garlic and chopped dill. Season with lemon zest and juice, salt, and pepper.
7. Discard any juice from the cucumber and mix the cucumber cubes with the yogurt.
8. Cut the beetroots into bite-size pieces, toss with olive oil, and season with salt and pepper.
9. Make a small 'mountain' of beetroot on a plate and top with the cucumbers. Sprinkle on freshly picked dill, finely grated lemon zest, and toasted pine nuts.

TIP: *You can use hazelnuts or almonds instead of pine nuts. If you don't have any beetroot, this dish also tastes heavenly with roasted carrots. You can find the recipe in this book.*

MASHED POTATOES
with HERBS

(G) (D) (N) (V)

1 kg potatoes
100-200 ml milk
50 ml olive oil
1/4 bunch fresh parsley
1/2 bunch fresh chives
1/2 bunch dill
1 handful fresh tarragon
Juice and zest of 2 lemons
1 small garlic clove, grated
Salt and pepper to taste

1. Scrub or peel the potatoes (if they are fresh summer potatoes, keep the skin on).
2. Boil the potatoes in unsalted water, turn down the heat to a simmer and cook until they are tender and can be easily mashed.
3. Place the herbs in a bowl and pour boiling water over them or blanch them for 1–2 seconds in a pot of boiling water. Rinse them immediately in cold water. Then, squeeze out the water and chop them roughly.
4. Blend the herbs with the grated garlic, oil, and 50 ml of milk using an immertion blender.
5. Drain the water from the potatoes and mash them roughly with a potato masher or a whisk.
6. Add the rest of the milk (warm) to soften the mixture a little and then stir in the olive oil mixture to add a beautiful green color. Season to taste with salt, pepper, and lemon zest and juice.

TIP: *You can use plant based milk.*

Easy

 2 people

 15 minutes

VEAL PICCATA

2 veal schnitzels (approx. 400 g)
50 g wheat flour or rice flour
2 tbsp. butter
150 ml white wine
350 ml chicken stock
(or 200 ml water and a bouillon cube)
2 lemons
50 g capers
1 small bunch parsley
Salt and pepper to taste
Olive oil

1. Cut 1 lemon into slices. Blanch the lemon slices to make them less bitter. Finely zest the rind from the other lemon and squeeze its juice into a bowl.
2. Chop the parsley.
3. Cut each schnitzel into two pieces and pound flat with a meat tenderizer or the back of a saucepan. Season with salt and pepper.
4. Toss the schnitzels in flour, dust off any excess flour and fry them in a pan with a little oil for approx. 1–2 minutes on each side until golden.
5. Place the schnitzels on a plate and cover with foil.
6. Add wine and lemon juice to the pan and deglace it. Reduce it by half.
7. Pour in the stock and bring it to a boil. Add the cold butter and combine into an emultion.
8. Add the capers, parsley, and lemon zest and slices and heat through. Season the sauce with lemon juice, salt, and pepper.
9. Serve with pasta or potatoes.

TIP: *You can also make the dish with chicken.*

Medium 1 cake

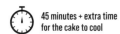45 minutes + extra time
for the cake to cool

Baked CHEESECAKE

(N) (V)

Bottom layer
225 g graham crackers
85 g butter, melted
1 pinch salt
1 springform pan (approx. 23 cm)

Top layer
450 g cottage cheese
200 g Greek yogurt
100 ml maple syrup
2 large eggs
1/2 pod of vanilla or 1 tsp vanilla essense
2 tbsp. corn starch
50 ml lemon, lime, or orange juice
2 lemons, limes, or oranges, zested
1 pinch salt
Fresh mint leaves (optional)

1. Preheat the oven to 170°C/340°F.
2. For the bottom layer, crush the biscuits into crumbs. You can use a mini chopper or put them in a plastic bag and pound them into pieces with a rolling pin.
3. Combine the crumbs with the salt and melted butter.
4. Press the mixture into a springform pan or tart tin. Press firmly at the bottom, possibly using the bottom of a small saucepan.
5. Bake for approx. 10 minutes, remove from oven, and let cool.
6. For the top layer, blend the cottage cheese, Greek yogurt, maple syrup, eggs, vanilla, lemon (or lime or orange) juice, finely grated zest, and salt in a blender until you have a smooth texture.
7. Pour the cheesemixture into the springform pan and bake for approx. 25–30 minutes or until the cake is firm and gel-like when you gently shake the tin.
8. Leave the cake to cool and then place it in the fridge for at least 1 hour.
9. Peel the orange and cut into slices; remove the seeds.
10. Serve the cake topped with the orange slices and possibly some fresh mint.

TIP: *Make the cake creamier: Replace the cottage cheese with cream cheese.*
You can also replace the maple syrup with 8 soft Medjool dates, chopped and blended with the eggs.
Or Add 85 g of brown sugar to the bottom crust recipe if you want it to be extra sweet.

GORKA PRIETO-BELLVER

"The riders are always hungry."

Sports nutritionist working for Team UAE Emirates

Gorka Prieto-Bellver is one of the most respected nutritionists in the cycling world. He is currently working with Team UAE Emirates and conducting research as part of a PhD focusing on cyclists and nutrition.

"I studied human nutrition in Spain. And then I've also done a Master's in food nutrition and training in Madrid. I have been working with cyclists since 2015. I'm doing a PhD about how we can improve performance with different types of diets. So now I'm doing research on that topic as part of the PhD."

What is the main philosophy behind the team's nutritional plan?

"We have different guidelines, depending on the ability of each driver. So, we need to draw distinctions between when they are home and when they are training. And then when we're racing, it's all about performance. It depends on the profile of the stage, it depends on the role of the rider. We have different targets in terms of proteins, lipids, and carbohydrates, depending on the riders weight, and depending on their role and what they need to complete, what they need to do based on the stage profile."

At the Tour de France, teams have eight riders, each with specific skills, ambitions, and roles to play during a stage; these roles might vary depending on the profile of the stage. This requires individual planning, he says.

"We perform an estimation that takes different things into account before each stage. We do an estimation of how much power they're going to make, and we do that with the head coach of the team. Depending on the role of the rider, we will also have a discussion with the Sport Director. They have different plans. And then there are plans for after the stage. Because if it's a flat stage, there could be a crosswind, and then the power required is quite high, so then the energy demand is also quite high. So we need to adjust what they are eating after the stage. Because if not, if they are under-fueling, the next day their performance might decrease."

Weighing food is the trend these days, but please talk us through a day of the Tour de France from a nutrition perspective.

"It is mandatory to weigh the food. I work quite closely with the chefs. They are fundamental, now, to performance. So, we have different recipes in the team that we create between the chefs and me, so they need to always make the same recipes with the same quantities, the same type of pasta with the same everything, always. We have different protocols, so there are different types of carbs available at breakfast for the rider. And it's up to them whether they take one kind of food or another, but they need to meet a target. It is something that they just know. If you want to take bread, for example, you know that you need to take 100 grams of bread, plus you should also take 500 grams of oat porridge or rice porridge or different carbs that we have at breakfast to meet the target, which should be, I don't know, 200 grams of carbs in total for the breakfast. It depends, and it's up to them. Because they have a lot of options. But we know, and they know, the amount of carbs per 100 grams of porridge, or the amount of carbs in this type of bread. Or how much is in three grams of syrup. So, they put the plate on the scale, and they throw on the food that they need to eat."

Weighing food to gather data and improve the riders' performances is a new thing, he says.

"Initially, when I joined the team, it was more like they didn't know, they didn't have a specific plan about eating carbs, or say that you need to eat carbs for performance. So that's what I've done

over the last four years. I've been trying to make a plan with the chefs to try to do the best we can to keep the weight stable, so they can recover as well as possible. And perform as well as possible, also, and each rider has a plan. And we are making an app just to make it easier for the riders, and I can send them a plan saying, 'Bernard, on Tuesday, you need to eat 500 grams of porridge, 100 grams of bread,' and then it's up to them whether or not to change something."

After a stage is complete, a new race begins: a race against time, to fuel the riders up and get them ready for the next day's stage.

"When they arrive at the finish line, they have a soda, like Fanta or Coca-Cola. They have different options. Also, they need to start rehydrating. We have water, sometimes with some salt, or just plain water at the finish line. They take a recovery meal, a recovery shake, but it's always with carbs and protein. You can put in more carbs, or you can give them some Haribo, because some like eating some solid food, and they also get a proper meal. It always has rice, or pasta, and something with protein as well – we have eggs, or some chicken breast, or some tuna. The quantity depends; it will change depending on how much power they have expended during this stage because it's quite important to start fueling again and get back the glycogen that they have lost during the ride. Because if the amount of power required is quite high, they're going to use a lot of glycogen. So that's the reason we try to start refueling properly, depending on how much power they have used."

The intake of various kinds of liquids and meals at the finish line is not only about hunger, but an actual race against time. There is a window after the riders finish during which they have to eat.

"We try to make sure they eat in the first 30 minutes, to start replenishing that glycogen. There have been a lot of theories on this. In the beginning, they were telling us that it's only 15 minutes, but then a lot of researchers found that that wasn't important. Again, the most important thing is the quantity, the timing. But also, in recent research, we have seen that is quite important to start eating right after you finish because the glycogen replenishment is going to be difficult."

What happens if a rider has food fatigue and cannot eat? What happens in terms of the recovery? How do they suffer if they don't eat within that window?

> *"The riders are always hungry after the finish line, and it is important to begin the refueling. They're always hungry. But at dinner, we have a problem getting them to eat like 6000 calories, or 7000 calories for big riders because they expend a lot of power. It's a struggle for them."*

"So you need to devise strategies and try to fuel early, because if you don't, the next day, they can be under-fueled and they'll just be dead, in terms of performance. And you need to try to do something tasty, too, to work with the cooks. It's important for us. In our team, we have really good chefs, so for us it's quite easy to fuel the riders."

When the riders are off-season, their diet and nutrition program is less strict and monitored.

"What I do is just check their training program. And we have differences, yes, between when they are at home and when they are racing. So,

when they are at home, they have their own plans, depending on the goal that they have. If the goal is just to lose weight, we need to restrict calories during a period. Then, depending on the training plan that they have, what I do is just send them a program based on the training. So, if the goal is just to lose weight, we need to restrict calories. And if the goal is just to gain weight, we need to increase calories in part of the program, but it's always going to be dependent on the training they have. Because for me, it doesn't work if you make them a general plan, it needs to be specific just to try to achieve the goals that they have. And then when we are racing, we need to try to match calories. Just to try to keep it stable and allow them to recover as well as possible, to perform as well as possible."

Eddy Merckx, a true Tour de France legend, was a big fan of steaks and fueled on huge amounts of beef. However, red meats are largely a no-go in the modern-day Tour de France, as Gorka Prieto-Bellver explains.

"So, red meat is something that we remove from the diet. Because it is quite difficult to digest. For that reason, we try to include white proteins, like fish, white fish, or chicken, turkey, something easy to digest. Because we try to also have good gut health. And for that reason, we need to have high-quality foods, trying to avoid, for example, red meat, so that they are not eating too much. They always complain a bit about that, saying okay, but we need red meat, we need red meat. But when it's a rest day, they can have it, or the day before a race day. We try to have an approach that's common sense, but not super strict, while also trying to promote good habits and good gut health for them."

How about a vegan diet? Is it possible to ride a Tour de France as a vegan: only consuming plant-based proteins? Can you physically eat enough and recover enough on a plant-based diet?

"It is possible, for sure. Because in the end, you can have different protein sources, like tofu, or training with seitan. We have chickpea protein. You have different options. And in the end, one rider, their weight is around 60 kilos. To achieve the protein intake that they need is quite easy, because it's quite low because they have low body weight. So I think the most important thing is just to focus on carbohydrates. You eat a bit of protein, eat tofu or protein powder, different dampening powders, and it's quite easy to achieve the amount that they should eat. So, it is 100 percent possible."

Gorka Prieto-Bellver makes sure to be a part of the preparations and camps for the Tour de France and the grand tour itself.

"Yeah, I always do Tour de France, and I'll always do training for the Tour de France. That's the most important thing, it's the race of the year. So we need to prepare well. We do gut training sessions. So, for that reason, I speak with the coach. And we reach an agreement - yes, okay, today we're going to do gut training sessions."

"So, I go with the service car, with the coach giving them food every 15 minutes. And we want to try to do a high carb intake in that particular training session because the goal is just to train your gut. So we do it like that, taking the calories into account because we know all the recipes, we know all the calories that they have in everything. We can train the gut with a lot of carbs, with 120 grams per hour, and then we can lose weight if that's the goal. For some riders, the goal is to just lose weight in that period, others just need to keep their weight stable. And it's not common, but sometimes they might need to gain weight. So, depending on the different goals that we have, we start preparing them from the training camp."

How do you see the future of nutrition within pro cycling over the next five to ten years? What do you think it's going to look like?

"I think it's just getting bigger and bigger, having more people – in terms of more nutritionists, more chefs and more structures, big structures to ensure we have good tracks. I think that we are improving every year when it comes to doing everything more accurately. I mean, that's the future of sport nutrition, doing everything, like measuring everything depending on how much power you've expended in each particular zone. So you know the amount of carbs you've burned during the stage, and you need to know the amount of carbs you need to fuel after the stage, you're more accurate in terms of everything. I think that's the future of sport nutrition, having more and more people involved in that particular area that nowadays, for sure, is a big part of performance."

STAGE 10

Easy

 4-6 people

 15 minutes

ROASTED CARROT
with LETTUCE
AND BLUEBERRIES

Ⓖ Ⓓ Ⓝ Ⓥ

Salad
600 g small carrots
2 heads mini romaine lettuce
100 g blueberries
2 tbsp. olive oil
Salt and pepper to taste

Dressing
100 ml olivenolie
1 tsk. sennepsfrø
1 spsk. ahornsirup
25 ml rødvinseddike
100 ml vand
1 skalotteløg
Salt og peber

1. Bring the mustard seeds to a boil in the water. Cover and let steep while everything else is being prepared.
2. Peel and finely mince the shallot.
3. Scrub or peel the carrots.
4. Cut the romaine lettuce heads into quarters.
5. Heat 1 tbsp. olive oil in a pan over medium-high heat. Then, fry the carrots over high heat so that they brown nicely. Season with salt.
6. Turn the heat down to medium and cook the carrots for 4–5 more minutes or until they are tender.
7. Remove the carrots from the pan and wipe the pan clean.
8. Fry the romaine lettuce in a little olive oil and salt for approx. 2 minutes on only one of the cut surfaces. The lettuce must be raw on one side.
9. Whisk the vinegar, maple syrup, and strained mustard seeds together with the Dijon mustard and season with salt and pepper.
10. Add the rest of the olive oil little by little and whisk it into the mixture. Season with salt, pepper, and, if necessary, a little maple syrup.
11. Arrange the carrots, romaine lettuce, and blueberries beautifully on a plate and pour the dressing over them.

TIP: *You can use any kinds of berries in season.*
Feel free to make a large portion of the dressing and store it in the fridge. The mustard seeds absorb a lot of flavor.

Easy

 4 people

 15 minutes

PASTA *with*
LEMON AND
MINT PESTO

3 organic lemons
1/2 bunch parsley
4 stalks fresh mint
1 small garlic clove
50 ml olive oil
50 g pine nuts
100 g parmesan or pecorino
Salt and pepper to taste
400 g spaghetti
1/2 tsp. chili flakes (optional)

1. Pick and roughly chop the herbs. Then, peel and finely chop the garlic.
2. Finely peel the lemons and finely slice the zest. Alternatively, you can use a fine zester.
3. Squeeze the juice from the lemons.
4. With a mini chopper, blend all the previously mentioned ingredients with the pine nuts, the olive oil, and half of the cheese. Season to taste with salt, pepper, and lemon juice and adjust the texture with a little extra water if necessary to obtain a smooth pesto.
5. Pour half of the pesto into a large bowl.
6. Cook the pasta in salted water according to the instructions on the bag.
7. Pour approx. 100 ml of pasta water into the bowl with the pesto and mix it in.
8. Strain the pasta, pour it into the bowl with the pesto, and mix everything together.
9. Serve the pasta dish topped with the rest of the cheese, the chili flakes (optional), and a handful of fresh herbs.

TIP: *You can use all kinds of fresh herbs for the pesto.*

Medium   4-6 people

 3 hours

PORK CHEEKS
(G) (N) *and* **POLENTA**

Pork cheeks

600 g pork cheek
2 onions
1 garlic clove
3 parsnips
200 g small tomatoes
40 g tomato paste [1 small can]
1 cinnamon stick
1 tbsp. sweet paprika [preferably smoked]
1 tsp. cumin
1/2 tsp. chili flakes [optional]
500 ml chicken stock
3 tbsp. sherry vinegar or red wine vinegar
Olive oil
200 g carrots
Salt and pepper to taste
Fresh parsley

Polenta

200 g polenta
1250 ml broth or water
100 g parmesan or similar cheese
2 tbsp. olive oil
Salt and pepper to taste

1. Preheat the oven to 170°C/340°F.
2. Clean and trim the pork cheeks.
3. Brown the pork cheeks in a sauté pan with a little olive oil and salt and then place them in a dutch oven or an oven-proof dish.
4. Peel the onions and cut them into quarters. Halve the garlic crosswise.
5. Peel and slice the parsnips.
6. Rinse the tomatoes and poke a hole in each of them with a small knife.
7. Arrange all vegetables around the pork cheeks in the dutch oven. Add the spices, tomato paste, stock, and vinegar. Season with salt and pepper. Bake covered for approx. 2 hours or until the pork cheeks are completely tender.
8. Peel the carrots and cut them into bite-size pieces; set aside.
9. Bring 1250 ml of broth or saltet water to boil for the polenta.
10. Whisk in the polenta a little at a time. Turn down the heat to low and whisk frequently while the polenta cooks, approx. 10–15 minutes. Season with salt and pepper and set aside.
11. Once done, take the pork cheeks out of the oven and, if necessary, boil to reduce and thicken the sauce. Season with salt and pepper.
12. Before serving, roast the carrots in a pan with a little oil and salt.
13. Whisk the polenta over medium heat with a little broth/water until it reaches the desired consistency. Add the olive oil and cheese. Whisk again and taste.
14. Serve the pork cheeks with the polenta, roasted carrots, and fresh parsley.

Easy 4 persons

 60 minutes

Potato POWER CAKE

200 g raw potato
100 g rhubarb
2 large eggs
80 ml acacia honey
2 bananas
2 tbsp. butter
2 tsp. baking soda
Juice and zest of 2 limes
1/2 tsp. salt
50 g almonds
80 g oatmeal
1/2 tsp. vanilla powder
or 1 tbsp. vanilla extract

1. Preheat the oven to 170°C/340°F.
2. Cut the potatoes into cubes and cut the rhubarb into small pieces approx. 1–1.5 cm thick.
3. Blend all ingredients, except for the rhubarb, in a food processor with the pulse function. The result must be grainy, not a watery puree, so keep an eye on it. If you don't have a food processor, cut the potato into the smallest cubes possible and use a blender instead; you can also grate the potato and blend the ingredients with an immersion blender.
4. Let the potato batter rest for five minutes for the oatmeal to absorb the moisture.
5. Line a pie tin with baking paper or grease it with butter and sprinkle it with nut or rice flour.
6. Fill the tin with the batter and level the surface with a wet dough scraper or spoon.
7. Press the rhubarb pieces into the cake.
8. Bake for 45–50 minutes or until golden brown and firm but spongy. Turn the cake tin once halfway through the baking time to ensure an evenly baked surface. If the cake feels very soft when you press it, it needs a few extra minutes in the oven.

TIP: *You can use any seasonal fruit in the cake and season with citrus zest of your choice.*

STAGE

(V) HERB GARDEN

1 bunch small carrots
1 bunch radish
1/2 bunch green asparagus
1/2 bunch fresh tarragon
1/2 bunch chives
1/2 bunch parsley
1 tbsp. Dijon mustard
1 tbsp. firm honey
2 tbsp. apple cider vinegar
400 g cottage cheese
1 slice rye bread
1 slice sourdough bread
50 g hazelnuts, shelled
2 tbsp. olive oil
Salt and pepper to taste

1. Bring a pot of salted water to a boil.
2. Clean the radishes, asparagus, and carrots. Leave their tops on. Peel the carrots and break the bottom of the asparagus.
3. Pick and blanch the fresh herbs in boiling water for 2–3 seconds. Shock them in ice cold water immediately. Then, squeeze out the water and roughly chop the herbs.
4. Blend the herbs with the Dijon mustard, honey, and cottage cheese into a beautiful green cream. Season with the apple cider vinegar, salt, and pepper. Feel free to fill a piping bag with the mixture and store it in the fridge.
5. Cut the bread into small cubes and chop it into crumbs using a mini chopper.
6. Heat the olive oil in a pan and fry the breadcrumbs over medium heat until crispy and golden brown. They must not burn. Once completely crispy, place the breadcrumbs on 3–4 layers of kitchen paper to absorb the oil. Season with salt.
7. Wipe the pan clean. Chop the hazelnuts in a mini chopper and toast them until golden in the pan. You can also roast them in the oven at 170°C/340°F.
8. Arrange the cottage cheese cream in small jars or glasses, stick the vegetables in the cream, and top with crispy bread-nut-crumble.

SALMON FISH CAKES *with* RED COLESLAW

(G) (D)

Fish cakes
400 g salmon fillet
1 tsp. salt
2 eggs
2 tbsp. wheat flour or oat flour
2 spring onions
1/2 tsp. freshly grated ginger
Zest of 1 lime
Oil for frying
Salt and pepper to taste

Red coleslaw
1/4 head red cabbage
1 red pepper
1 apple
1/4 bunch mint
25 g pistachios
1 tbsp. honey/maple syrup
Juice and zest of 1 lemon
1 tbsp. olive oil
Salt and pepper to taste

1. Mince the salmon and salt in a food processor until smooth. If you don't have a food processor, you can chop the fish fillet and mix it well with the salt by hand or with a hand mixer.
2. Add the eggs and flour and mix until the dough has a firm consistency.
3. Pick and chop half of the mint. Finely chop the spring onion and finely grate the ginger.
4. Stir the ginger, spring onion, and lime zest into the mince and season with salt and pepper.
5. Fry a mini fish cake in olive oil in a pan. Have a taste and add more salt, pepper, or lime zest to the mince if necessary. Once you are satisfied with the taste, leave the mince to rest for 15 minutes while you make the salad.
6. Cut the red cabbage and pepper into thin strips, preferably using a mandolin.
7. Dice the apple and chop the pistachios.
8. Mix the lemon zest, juice, honey, and olive oil together. Season with salt and pepper and toss with the chopped vegetables, fruits, pistachios, and mint.
9. Arrange the coleslaw on a plate and top with mint, placing the fish cakes on the side.

NOTE: *The cakes can also be made with cod fish. However, it is recommended to replace the milk with cream, as cod is quite lean and the cod fish cakes could be a little dry otherwise.*

NOT a TIME TRIAL
PASTA RAGÙ

400 g diced beef
(preferably shank or bow)

200 g diced pork neck

2 onions

4 celery stalks

4 large carrots

4 garlic cloves

4 sprigs fresh rosemary

5 bay leaves, preferably fresh

200–300 ml wine
(white or red can be used)

80 g tomato puree (1 large can)

2 cans good-quality peeled
tomatoes

300 ml broth or water

2 tbsp. dried tarragon

1 tbsp. dried basil

1 tbsp. dried oregano

100 ml milk or cream

100 ml olive oil

Salt and pepper to taste

White wine vinegar

Grated peccorino

1. Brown the meat in a pan and set aside.
2. Rinse and finely cut all the fresh vegetables. You can grate the carrots or cut them into chunks and process them in a food processor until you have a granule-like mass – it must not be a puree!
3. In a large braising pot, sauté all the greens (except for the tomatoes) with a little olive oil over medium-high heat until tender. Season with salt and pepper.
4. Add all the spices and the tomato puree and cook for 1–2 minutes.
5. Pour in the wine and reduce to 1/3 of the original volume (deglaze).
6. Add in the browned meat, tomatoes, and broth or water. Season with salt and pepper and bring to a boil.
7. Turn the heat down to low. Cover the pot with a lid and let simmer, stirring regularly, for 3 hours. Add a little extra liquid along the way to ensure that the meat is always covered.
8. Once the meat is tender and falling apart, reduce the liquid, uncovered, until it reaches the desired thickness.
9. Remove the bay leaves and rosemary stems and season the dish with salt, pepper, and possibly a little bit of white wine vinegar.
10. Use two forks to pull the meat apart; if in a hurry, use an immersion blender to quickly pull it apart with 7–8 pulses.
11. Serve with freshly cooked pasta and grated pecorino (or a similar cheese).

TIP: *You can cook the dish in the oven at 165°C/330°F. Simply place the pan in the oven after step 6.*
You can make this dish in a pressure cooker. After step 6, the dish must have approx. 25 minutes under pressure. Once cooked, reduce the liquids to about ½ and season with salt and pepper.

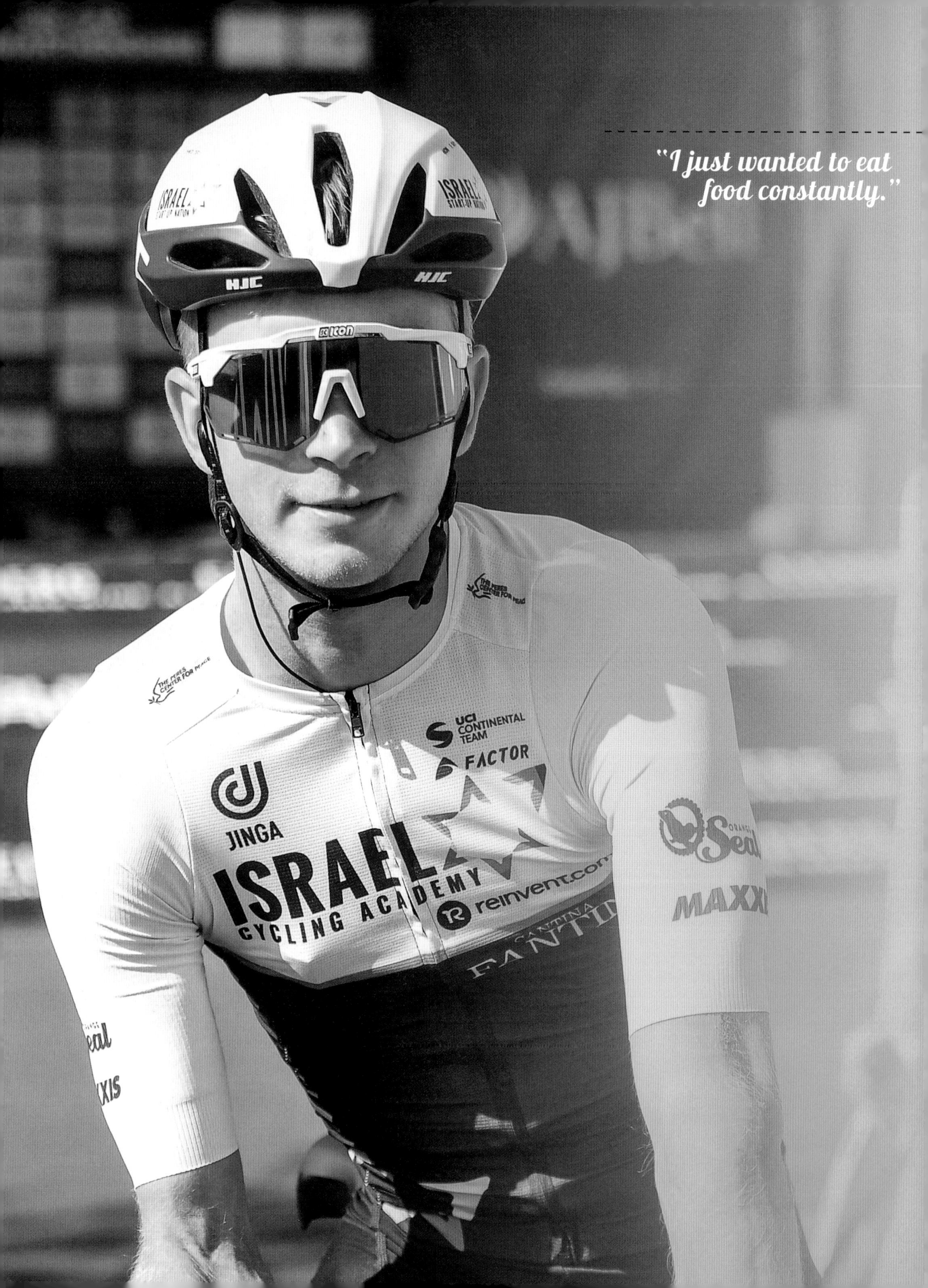

"I just wanted to eat food constantly."

MASON HOLLYMAN

Pro rider since 2021

Mason Hollyman has been a pro rider for a few years and has an exciting future ahead of him. Nutrition is no new concept to him, as he developed an interest in healthy foods as a teenager.

"I grew up in Yorkshire, Great Britain, close to Huddersfield. Cycling enthusiasts will be familiar with Hornfirth, located just north of the Peak District. It's quite a small village. I think around 3,000–4,000 people live there. There wasn't much to do there when I was a kid. The entire village had only one store and one pub, showing how small the town was. So yeah, I mean, obviously out of boredom, I took a classic British walk down the football lane at school. I was never the best footballer, to be honest. I didn't quite have the hand-eye coordination to be a football player. From there, I was introduced to cycling by my dad, who had always been a keen cyclist. He loved cycling and used to race a little in his free time, never like a pro cyclist, and still worked simultaneously. He used to take my brother and me out on little rides around where we lived. It was quite nice to ride around there. Minus the weather."

Most teenagers crave burgers and pizza every day, but not Mason Hollyman. He says his parents taught him at a young age to think and eat healthily, sometimes with a diet that most teenagers hate.

"I've always been interested in nutrition. I wouldn't say as young as 10 years old, but rather around 14 or 15 years old. I've always cared a lot about my diet and what I put in my body. And since I come from a family that is quite healthy, it was quite easy to learn this habit. My parents wanted me and my brother to grow up with a healthy eating lifestyle, so, you know, they made sure we had a nice, balanced diet. This is quite funny, but I recall that I hated breakfast when I was about 10 or 12 years old and didn't know why. Everyone claims that breakfast is their favorite meal of the day, but for some reason, I despise it. My mom was determined to do anything to get me to eat in the morning, so she'd give me food combinations like cheddar cheese, some slices of ham, and olives for breakfast."

His eating struggle, however, did not stop at breakfast. He had other eating issues, such as not wanting to eat during his training sessions, but he overcame them and found his way around them.

"I went through a rough food phase when I was younger. I hated eating when cycling. It was always a struggle for me. I preferred a brunch bar, a classic British brunch bar, or a Nature Valley bar, which was always a big choking hazard, to real food."

"And obviously, a banana – you can't beat a banana, sometimes, you know. They were my classics and go-to food replacements. And then, a few years later, I started making my snacks like flapjacks, especially peanut butter flapjacks, because they were always a favorite of mine. It was nice and calorific, and it boosted my energy while riding. I guess with age comes hunger as well. So, naturally, as soon as I became a teenager, I realized I just gravitated toward food and wanted to eat constantly. And just like that, I didn't struggle with food anymore. Since then, I have always had a shake after training. It's just a standard recovery shake, and I always have it with milk, which makes it taste more like a milkshake. I'm a massive fan of the way it tastes. So, yeah, I guess I've been relatively healthy since that phase of my life. After that, I began to expand my palate to other foods. My go-to meal then was wholemeal rice, tuna with chopped tomatoes, a bit of cheese on top, which was always good for me, and maybe a bit of hot sauce. The local cycling club members would give me food tips. They would tell me to eat or drink a bottle every hour or something like that. My dad had a decent understanding of healthy foods and things of that sort, so naturally, I was also interested in them. So yeah, I liked reading up on a healthy food lifestyle. I mainly wanted to read what cyclists like Chris Froome were eating."

When training on his own, Mason Hollymon does not eat a big breakfast before he rides.

"When I wake up, the first thing I do is try not to spike my insulin levels because I think about how quickly I'll be burning calories, so I lower my sugar intake to start the day to avoid it from spiking later. This keeps my metabolism firing up, and from there, I guess, maybe just before I ride, I can have a bit of something; say, if I'm riding at 9, 9:30, or 10, I might have a late breakfast. Once I've had a bit of food in my stomach, I head out. I sometimes deliberately do not eat; that way, I can stop at the cafe halfway through my training and eat whatever I want there. I think if you follow my routine and time it right, you can eat a big slice of cake and burn the calories by the time you get home. To me, the cafe is the perfect place to treat yourself. And yeah, I'd say that I have a nice dinner in the evening, but nothing crazy sugary again to avoid an insulin spike. I'd say that, in the last year or so, insulin is something I've looked at a lot. And I think that being cautious about it seems to be pretty useful."

"Despite only being a pro rider for a few years, I have noticed how my team's nutrition strategy has changed significantly in a very short time."

"It's a lot stricter when it comes to eating. I have never weighed my food before. Now I measure how many grams of carbs are in my food. Certainly, weighing what I eat has made a significant difference. Normally, you know, you just add more food. To be fair, for the last few years, I just ate as much as I could. Obviously, you know, that's just the way elite sport is; I think any advantage you can get with food is beneficial."

How about the menu for a full day of racing? What does it look like?

"I like to keep it the same every day. So, I go in with porridge, which the chef likes to change up, making it nice and slightly different each time. I don't know if cinnamon or something else is either cold or warm. I do not care. I add maybe some dark chocolate in there – 80–85%, maybe 20 grams of dark chocolate – and then I'd go in with maybe a little bit of honey and, of course, some berries – raspberries, blueberries, blackberries – and I sometimes have the porridge with a ham and cheese omelet, two eggs, and a lot of Riza rice. Yeah, nice bit of rice, but otherwise, I try and keep it quite plain; maybe if we are talking about day seven of a race, I'd have a bit of ketchup with it. I like my coffee decaffeinated in the morning and then caffeinated on the bus just before the race. I try not to overdo the caffeine. I mean, I could easily have ten coffees before I race, but I try to keep it a bit low until the last few days of racing when I start to feel tired."

Just before and during a race, Mason Hollyman eats various snacks to stay fueled.

"Normally, I eat a banana before I start cycling, or I have something light, like a nice, sweet bread. I don't really like feeling heavy at the start of a race, so I try not to overeat. I stuff a few chocolate or sweet bread snacks into my pockets before I start a race, a few slices kind of thing, especially the cakey-style types with chocolate chips in them, so yeah, that's always a good start. If it's going to be a long race, I might take two rice cakes and probably one more bar of chocolate at the most. Mostly, those snacks keep me powered during the first half of my race, and for the second half, I snack on gels. Yeah, depending on how hard the race is, I'll have like four to six gels, so I'll probably smash around 100–120 carbs in a race. I just like eating food. I think that's the trick to being a better athlete. Of course, it's not all about eating; there are various mixes and things that my team does to keep us fit. It is super easy now that we have these, to get enough carbs down."

After the race, it is the same procedure as the day before, Mason Hollyman says, with very few changes.

"After the race, I get off my bike and immediately take a recovery shake, head to the locker room and have a shower, get back to my room, get changed, and then straight to eating rice, maybe with a bit of chicken or an omelet, depending on what the chef decides. I usually top that off with a variety of sauces. My go-to sauce is usually Sriracha, but I don't use it daily. I change it up a bit every day. Normally, when I don't feel like eating Sriracha sauce, I replace it; I go the Chinese-style route and add a bit of soy sauce."

Then I'll go back to my room and get a massage. By dinnertime, I usually have a big appetite and rely on carbs for refueling.

"I prefer pasta, which normally comes with some pasta sauce. It's quite plain most times if the hotel is cooking; it just adds some pasta sauce and hopefully a bit of nice Parmesan."

"I believe that good parmesan and well-cooked rice can satisfy. If you get some slightly soggy rice and not the best Parmesan, then it's

just not the same. However, if you have some al dente Italian pasta and some good Parmesan on hand, it makes for an ideal combination."

"And obviously, I have chicken breast or something like a chocolate brownie with a nice scoop of vanilla ice cream afterward. You know what they say – the healthiest dessert is nothing. Before bedtime, I probably just eat yogurt topped with fruit. Something like that, maybe a bit of honey. I don't like too much sugar before bed because I don't want to be weird when I'm trying to sleep at night."

Mason Hollyman does not track his sleep, but getting many hours of sleep makes a huge difference to him.

"I am a huge fan of sleep. So, for me, eight to ten hours of sleep is important. I don't actually track it, but I can roughly guess what time I turn my lights off. Maybe in the future, I'll start tracking it. But I mean, yeah, I just try to relax and turn my phone off a bit before I go to bed. So, I'm not as tired, I'm more relaxed, and hopefully, I'll be able to fall asleep faster and avoid disrupting the quality of my sleep."

STAGE 12

Easy

 2 people

 20 minutes

CHICKPEA CURRY *with*

 FRIED SPRING ONIONS

G N V

1 can chickpeas
1 onion
1 garlic clove
1 tbsp. fresh ginger
1 tbsp. curry powder
1 tsp. cumin
2 tbsp. oil
200 ml yogurt
Juice of 1 lemon
1 bunch spring onions
1/2 bunch fresh mint
Salt and pepper to taste

1. Drain the chickpeas.
2. Peel and finely chop the onion and garlic. Grate the ginger.
3. Clean the spring onions.
4. Heat 1.5 tbsp. olive oil in a sauté pan and toast the curry and cumin over medium-high heat.
5. Add the onion, garlic, and ginger and sauté for approx. 2–3 minutes or until tender and translucent.
6. Add the chickpeas and heat through. Season with salt.
7. Remove the sauté pan from the heat and add the yogurt. Season to taste with salt and lemon juice.
8. Heat a frying pan over high heat, add 1/2 tbsp. olive oil, and fry the spring onions until tender, with a nice color. Season with salt.
9. Finely chop the mint.
10. Arrange the chickpeas in a large dish and top with spring onions and fresh mint. Serve with freshly cooked rice.

TIP: *You can also use beans or lentils for this dish.*

Easy   4-6 people

75 minutes

ROASTED CAULIFLOWER
(G) (N) (V) *with* YOGURT SAUCE

1 head cauliflower
3 tbsp. olive oil
2 tsp. garam masala
1 tsp. turmeric
1 tsp. cumin
Zest and juice of 1 lemon
250 ml yogurt
1/2 bunch mint, finely chopped
1 tin chickpeas
1 bunch spring onions
1/2 bunch coriander
1 clove of garlic
Salt and pepper to taste

1. Preheat the oven to 200°C/390°F.
2. Clean the cauliflower and cut a thin slice off the bottom if it is brown and dry.
3. Mix all of the spices and the lemon zest and juice in a bowl with the oil. Season with salt and pepper.
4. Place the cauliflower in a small ovenproof dish or oven-safe frying pan. Pour 50 ml of water into the bottom of the pan.
5. Cover with foil and bake for approx. 25 minutes.
6. Remove the foil. Use a spoon to pour the liquid from the bottom of the pan over the cauliflower and bake for another 40 minutes or until golden.
7. Mix the yogurt with the finely chopped mint, grated garlic, and lime juice and zest and season with salt.
8. Serve the cauliflower with the yogurt sauce and fresh mint.

TIP: *You can add boiled chickpeas or white beans, sliced onions, and sliced peppers to the bottom of the baking dish for the last 25 minutes and serve with rice for a vegetarian main course. Remember to give it a little splash of olive oil and season with salt and pepper.*

(G) (N) BUTTER CHICKEN

Chicken

400 g chicken
Juice and zest of 1 lemon
200 ml yogurt
2 tbsp. garam masala
1 garlic clove
Salt and pepper to taste

Sauce

2 onions
1 bulb ginger the size of a golf ball
3 garlic cloves
1 tbsp. garam masala
1 tsp. ground cumin
1 tsp. ground coriander
1 can tomato paste (40 g)
1 can peeled and diced tomatoes
1/2 tsp. chili powder (optional)
1.5 tsp. fine salt
250 ml coconut milk or cream
(e.g., plant-based oat cream)
125 ml stock
2 tbsp. olive oil
25 g almonds, chopped
25 g raisins

1. Cut the chicken into 3 × 3 cm cubes.
2. Mix the finely grated lemon zest and juice, yogurt, garam masala, finely grated garlic, salt, and pepper into a marinade.
3. Toss the chicken in the marinade and let sit for at least 1 hour or preferably overnight in the fridge.
4. For the sauce, peel the onion and garlic and chop finely. Grate the ginger coarsely.
5. Preheat the oven to 175°C/345°F.
6. Heat the olive oil in a pan and sauté the onion, garlic, and ginger until tender and translucent over medium heat.
7. Add the dried spices. Season with salt and pepper. (You can omit chili powder here if you don't want the dish to be spicy.)
8. Add the tomato paste and fry for 1–2 minutes.
9. Add the peeled tomatoes and stock and bring to a boil. Then, turn down the heat and let simmer for 5–7 minutes until everything is completely tender.
10. Transfer to a blender and blend the sauce until smooth. Season with salt and possibly a little more garam masala or chili.
11. Pour the sauce back into the pan. Add the chopped almonds and the raisins and let simmer over low heat while the chicken cooks.
12. Evenly distribute the chicken on a baking sheet lined with baking paper and bake for approx. 10–12 minutes or until the chicken is cooked but still juicy.
13. Add the coconut milk to the sauce and heat it through. Then add the chicken and season with the juice from the oven tray with the chicken so that you get a good acidity and sweetness balance.
14. Serve with rice and fresh coriander.

Easy

 1 cake

 60 minutes

THE *yellow* TOUR CAKE

(G) (D) (V)

100 ml applesauce
100 ml flavor-neutral oil
100 ml maple syrup
130 ml plant-based yogurt
2 eggs
Juice and zest of 2 lemons
100 g pitted Medjool dates, chopped
60 g rolled oats
70 g rice flour
70 g cashews
1/2 tsp. salt
1 tsp. ground turmeric
1 tsp. freshly grated ginger
2 pears
1 tsp. baking soda

Poaching liquid
100 ml water
100 ml white wine
2 tbsp. honey
½ tsp ground turmeric

1. Blend the wet ingredients (excluding the poaching liquids) along with the turmeric, ginger, and chopped dates into a smooth pure.
2. Mix the rest of the dry ingredients in a mixing bowl and combine with the pure.
3. Peel the pears. Cut one into cubes and fold the cubes into the batter.
4. Cut the second pear into small wedges. Bring the poaching liquid ingredients to a boil and poach the pear in the liquid.
5. Grease a cake tin and dust with rice flour on the bottom and sides.
6. Pour the batter in and bake the cake for 40–45 minutes or until golden brown and firm. Remember to turn the cake tin halfway through the baking time.
7. Let cool before serving. Serve topped with poached pear wedges.

TIP: *You can use any type of fruit in this cake. You can also make muffins with the batter.*

STAGE 13

POLKA dot COLESLAW

(G) (D) (N) (V)

Salad
1 fennel
1 courgette
1 kohlrabi
50 g red currants

Dressing
250 ml liquid tahini
Juice and zest of 2 lemons
100 ml water
2 tbsp. maple syrup or honey
2 tbsp. olive oil
1 small garlic clove
Salt and pepper to taste

1. For the salad, clean all greens.
2. Cut off the brown bottom of the fennel and cut the fennel into thin slices across the veins, use a Japanese mandolin for the best results.
3. Peel the kohlrabi and julienne it using a Japanese mandolin or grate it roughly.
4. Cut the courgette into thin strips. Feel free to use a Japanese mandolin or thin peeler.
5. For the dressing, whisk the tahini with the lemon zest and juice. Then, whisk in the water a little at a time until you have a creamy texture.
6. Whisk in the maple syrup, olive oil, and finely grated garlic and season with salt, pepper, and possibly more maple syrup to taste.
7. Toss the cut greens with half of the dressing and season with salt and pepper.
8. Arrange on a plate and top with the red currants. Serve the rest of the dressing on the side.

TIP: *You can use any crisp greens in the salad. Add apples or pears for a nice sweet crisp touch.*

Easy

 4 people

 30 minutes

"BÉARNAISE" POTATO SALAD

(G) (D) (N) (V)

Salad
1 kg potatoes
1 red onion
50 g capers
100 g cornichons
1/2 bunch fresh tarragon
Salt and pepper to taste

Vinaigrette
2 tbsp. apple cider vinegar
2 tbsp. Dijon mustard
2 tbsp. honey
1 tsp. salt
200 ml olive oil

1. Bring the potatoes to a boil in lightly salted water. Turn down the heat and let simmer for 10 minutes. Remove the pot from the heat and let the potatoes finish cooking in the hot water for about 10 minutes. If your potatoes are very large the cooking time will be longer and vice versa.
2. Peel the red onion and cut a few thin slices. Place in a bowl and pour apple cider vinegar over them.
3. Finely chop the rest of the red onion, capers, cornichons, and tarragon. Feel free to use a mini chopper.
4. Whisk together all the vinaigrette ingredients and season with salt and pepper.
5. Toss the capers mix with the vinaigrette.
6. Drain the potatoes and cool them down in cold water. Cut them into bite-size pieces and toss them together with the vinaigrette. Season to taste with salt and pepper.
7. Arrange in a bowl and top with fresh tarragon leaves and the lightly pickled onion slices.

TIP: *This potato salad is DEEEEELICIOUS and it gets even better if you make it a day ahead.*

Easy

 4-6 people

50 minutes
+ at least 1 hour (optional)

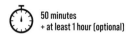 # BBQ CHICKEN

1 can tomato paste (80 g)

1 tbsp. smoked paprika

1 tbsp. ground cumin

50 ml apple cider vinegar
or white wine vinegar

100 ml maple syrup or honey

3 tbsp. olive oil

4-6 whole chicken thighs

Salt and pepper to taste

1. Mix the tomato paste, smoked paprika, cumin, apple cider vinegar, maple syrup, and olive oil together. Season with salt and pepper.
2. Divide the chicken thighs in half, into the upper and lower thighs.
3. Coat the chicken in the marinade. Try to get the marinade under the skin to give the meat as much flavor as possible.
4. Let the chicken marinate for at least 1 hour or overnight in the fridge to become even richer in taste.
5. Preheat the oven to 160°C/320°F.
6. Place the chicken in an ovenproof dish. Bake for 45–50 minutes or until cooked through, juicy, and tender.
7. Serve with salt 'n vinegar potatoes.

How to:
CUT A CHICKEN

1. Place the chicken on a cutting board, breast side up.
2. Cut the wings from the body by cutting through the joint at the chest.
3. Cut the thighs from the body by cutting through the skin where the thigh attaches. Bend the legs back so that the femur pops out and then cut through the joint to cut the thigh free.
4. Separate the upper thighs from the lower thighs by cutting through the joint where you can feel them bend. If you hit it right, the knife will slide right through.
5. Place the ribcage breast side down and cut it into two equal halves through the sternum with a sharp knife.
6. Cut each breast free from the ribs with a sharp knife.
7. You can further divide each breast piece into two parts as shown on the right.

REMEMBER: Always pat the chicken skin dry with a paper towel before roasting it in the oven, as the skin will be crispier.

ROAST A WHOLE CHICKEN – DELICIOUS AND JUICY:

1. Preheat the oven to 160°C/320°F.
2. Season the chicken with salt and pepper and place it on a small baking sheet. Let it rest at room temperature while the oven heats up.
3. Pat the skin dry, grease it with oil, and season it again with salt and pepper.
4. Roast the chicken for 1 hour.
5. Remove from the heat and let the chicken rest for approx. 15 minutes before cutting into it.

TIP: Store the chicken scraps and bones in the freezer to make your own chicken stock.

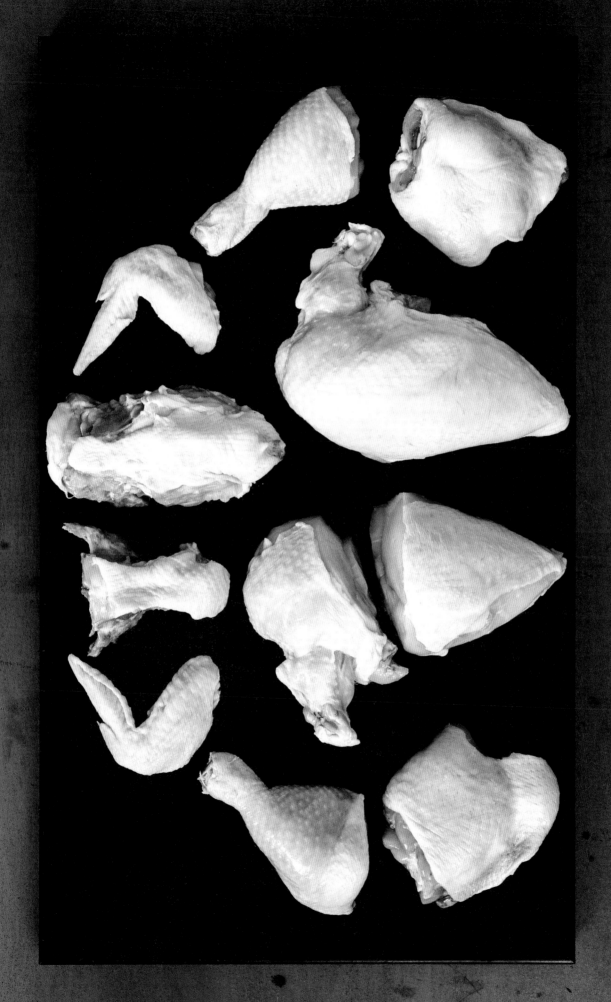

Easy | 4-6 people

40-45 minutes

SALT'N'VINEGAR

(G) (D) (N) (V) **POTATOES**

1 kg potatoes
2 tbsp. apple cider vinegar
2 tbsp. olive oil
Salt and pepper to taste
Olive oil

1. Preheat the oven to 215°C
2. Peel or scrub the potatoes and cut them into bite-size pieces.
3. Mix olive oil and 1 tbsp. vinegar together and toss the potatoes in the mix. Season with salt and pepper.
4. Spread the potatoes on a baking tray lined with baking paper and roast them in the oven for 30–35 minutes or until they are completely crispy and thoroughly roasted. Turn them around on the tray regularly whilst they roast.
5. Before serving, toss the potatoes with the rest of the vinegar and season with salt and possibly more vinegar to taste.

TIP: *Season the potatoes with paprika and chili. You can also add fresh or dried herbs at the end, such as dill, basil, or oregano.*

Easy

 12 cakes

 35-40 minutes

RASPBERRY ORANGE *cakes*

(G) (D) (V)

2 medium-size bananas
2 eggs
160 g pitted Medjool dates (approx. 12)
60 g peanut butter or almond butter
½ tsp. salt
1 tsp. vanilla powder or essence
1 tsp. ground cardamom
1 orange
45 g butter/coconut oil
100 g coconut flour
100 g oat flour (blended oatmeal)
1 tsp. baking soda
1 tsp. baking soda
100 g raspberries
50-100 ml water

1. Preheat the oven to 170°C/340°F.
2. Chop the dates and mash the bananas.
3. Blend the dates, bananas, nut butter, and eggs. If you don't have a food processor, use an immersion blender or a whisk to mash everything together.
4. Add all the dry ingredients (except the raspberries) and the finely grated orange zest to the mixture and combine well.
5. Whisk in the melted butter and gently fold in the raspberries – save a few for decoration.
6. Place the paper cups in a muffin tin and spread the batter evenly until each cup is 3/4 full.
7. Bake for approx. 20–25 minutes or until golden brown and firm.
8. Let cool a bit before serving.

TIP: *You can use any type of fruit in the recipe; just make sure to cut it into small cubes.*
Mix different spices to taste. You can, for example, make a Christmas spice mixture with cloves, cinnamon, and powdered ginger.
You can store your muffins in the fridge for 3–4 days or in the freezer for up to 3 months.

VOIGT & STEPHENS

"We had jelly and Mars bars."

Jens Voigt is one of the most well-liked Peloton riders in the history of the Tour de France. Always hard-working but with a smile on his face, he was celebrated and loved by fans and teammates. For 17 years, he was the record holder of racing the Tour de France. Now retired, he describes how nutrition and understanding of food have changed over the years and how Italian pasta is always perfect, but French pasta sometimes struggles. But first, let's hit the time machine button and return to where it all began for Jens Voigt in former East Germany.

"I was nine years old, and I guess in all honesty, I was a little bit of a troublemaker in school. I talked too much, I moved too much, and I always had a lot of energy. I could not sit still. So, I distracted the other kids, and then the teacher went to my parents and said, 'Hey, Mr. and Mrs. Voight, your kid has too much energy; he needs to do some sports.'"

"It was fortunate that I lived back in East Germany in the old days, as they just said 'He's a wild child; we can do sport and burn off that extra energy., we can do sport and burn off that extra energy. If I were the same child today, they would probably diagnose me withfive different mental defects and sending me to therapies until I actually did turn crazy."

Like Jens Voigt, Matt Stephens is a former pro-rider, popular pundit, and commentator. Working first as a pro-rider and then as a pundit, he has seen the transition and change in understanding nutrition through the decades like few other riders. First, another ticket for the time machine.

"We are going back a long, long time. We should have this zoom call in black and white, really. I was born in North London in 1970. I'm 53 now as we speak, so, pretty much for the vast majority of my life, since I was about 15 years old, cycling has been everything to me. I've been involved in the cycling world in various capacities for the best part of 35–40 years."

Speaking of training and nutrition and the changes that have taken place, Matt Stephens says, "I'm quite traditional in many ways, but the modernity of the sport, from the tech to the aesthetics of everything and down to the nutrition and training now, is just mind-blowing. When I started out, fueling on your bike was so basic. I remember most of my winter rides when I was 16, 17, and 18, were with my mum's fruitcake in my back pocket wrapped in some Bako foil. And jelly. Not jam, but jelly. The little cubes of jelly

Jens Voigt
Professional(pro)-rider 1998–2014

we would fuel with because there were no gels invented. So, we had our jelly and Mars bars."

There was no discussion about nutrition for either former rider when they were young. Voigt and the other children in East Germany were fueled by whatever their parents served for dinner along with a small slice of cake to eat before the races.

"Kids' racing is like you are letting go of a horde of sheep, or whatever. Everybody just goes full gas at the start, so the start is more or less everything. Five to 10 minutes into the race, positions don't really change anymore. If you're in the 10th position, you'll probably stay there. If you're in the lead, you might finish second or third, but you're not going to drop down to the 20th position. So, the start is crucial at kids' racing because it is just unorganized. There are no tactics, and it's full gas as long as you can. You've got to have energy in the tank right from the beginning. A piece of sugary cake could make all the difference."

Matt Stephens, little by little, gained some experience in nutrition and food. How? From learning by doing.

"Jelly was bizarrely quite modern, and it was very cheap. It was like 10 pence for a little box of jelly. Take the cardboard off, and it was in plastic. And it is delicious and has really high sugar content, so its just like a gel. But we didn't know really what we were doing, you know?"

"Back then, nutrition was based on taking things like sandwiches from the house and just eating them on the bike. There was no specialism at all. I think it took me a couple of years to work out that I didn't need an enormous, cooked break-fast. As I got older, I realized that you needed to eat well after your ride and have a good dinner. Then in the morning, not a massive breakfast, just a good, medium to small breakfast would be enough followed by fueling evenly."

"But when I was young, if I was going out on a long 160 km ride, I would eat until I could hardly move then go out and ride and not eat anything again, really, until I blew. And then it's like, 'Oh, now I need to go to a garage.' So, it would just be these spikes."

When Jens Voigt became a pro-rider, he prefer-red hot baguettes with butter and jam, which was a common thing to eat. Gradually, food became a focal point for the pro-teams. Chefs were hired, and later, food trucks became a familiar sight. But when did it all change?

"I would say I started in 1998. And five years later, we would have a chef, at least at the big races like Paris Nice, Criterium du Dauphiné in June, and then the Tour de France."

"Because then, if there was a longer transfer, you could send half of the team straight to eat, and the other ones would go to massage first, and then you would swap around."

"So, the chef would be, 'Okay, at eight, I feed five riders, and at nine, I feed the other four after the massage session,' so it would be more efficient, and the food would be nice, warm, and ready, and it would look good. Then, about seven years into my career, we saw the introduction of food trucks. Because as you may know, cooks don't like strangers in their kitchen for whatever reason. You know, they don't like that. So, it is obviously a discussion. It's a lot easier to just have a long electric cable, plug it in, and cook everything in your truck because then you can do whatever you want. You can park the truck, and you can start cooking at noon, or 4pm, or whatever you want. You can even make your own bread by that time."

Matt Stephens remembers the nineties with mixed feelings. Teams became more aware of the effects of nutrition.

"There were lots and lots of changes, especially in the mid-90s, I would say in terms of nutrition and training. From the time of Chris Boardman and Peter Keen, and then with Dave Brailsford in the early noughties, the British became, they became the world leaders in all that sort of thing. From being a country that was almost, well, really out on the periphery, Great Britain, as a cycling nation, became a powerhouse. Basically, from from 1992 through to late 2000, those eight years saw dramatic change. And I was part of that. I saw that happen and learned a lot. I was coached for the first time and learned a hell of a lot about training and nutrition and the importance of it. And as you can see, performances changed."

However, teams were still obsessed with the weight of the riders but with no proper or scientific control.

"I did experiment with different ways of losing weight. And even in the 90s, we knew that we had to be light. I mean, you could measure power, but only on a static rig at that particular time, as it wasn't till the late 90s that you could actually have the SRM on a bike. So fundamentally, people wanted to be light. I was in a French team, and their dietary methods were very, very strange. They had their ideas of what had fat in it. They wouldn't let us eat tomato ketchup, for example, but they were happy for us to have camembert at the end of a meal, that sort of psychology."

"So basically, I knew that I had to get lighter. I was very young when I joined ACDB20. And you're still not fully formed as a man. You're growing, your bone structure is slightly different, and your musculature is different."

"And I was called out for being overweight. If you look at the pictures back then, I was so skinny, but they said I was still fat, and it was just because I wasn't ripped. Psychologically, not eating is enormously damaging. It was damaging that

I had my breakfast at midnight then went out in the morning fasting. I did that for about a year."

Matt Stephens did experience some changes, but it took a while, particularly regarding cultural understanding.

"So back then, it was going out for a ride and sweating out a cold. For three years on every training camp in France, I had a bad chest infection. But they would tell me to take vitamin C and ride and sweat the cold out. It is like, 'What?'"

"So, there is that. And then there was a thing about not drinking on a bike because if you get used to not drinking, it'll make your body better. And then if you can't get a bottle out on a bike race, you're going to be even better. Some riders would train and not take a drink for four hours. So when you get home, you'd be pissing custard or nothing at all."

"So, there's all this stuff that was taken from the bygone era that took quite a few years to finally pull away from. And as you just pointed out, right at the very beginning, there are still some teams with different outlooks. Nowadays, you can be selective, and there's different cultures within teams, because it's so scientific now we're getting towards the point where we know what's right and wrong. When you factor in different human physiologies, demands, and environments, there is a good way of doing it. I guess there are still a few arguments, but looking at what we did, it was so traditional. Before we knew about science in the Middle Ages, in a very simplistic term, it was just, 'We don't really understand nutrition, and this is how we've done it, so this is the way we're going to continue doing it.' The change was very slow in France, for example."

All riders have their "war stories" from the races about crashes, broken bones, and scars, but when it comes to food, it's just food, right?

"Not at all," says Jens Voigt, who still remembers horror stories from the dinner table about how the food at the races changed.

"Here's one example you can talk to anybody of my generation of riders about. If you race in France, you'll be in a French hotel, let's say a Campanile hotel. If they then call the hotel, the race organizer goes, 'Hey, these bike riders, they come and want to eat their pasta with meat at 8 pm.' Remember 8 pm! The French would throw their pasta in the water at noon, at bloody noon. They would cook the pasta for eight hours every single time, every single day. It would just be soggy and full of water. And more than once we said, 'Hey, chef! Do you see the food? Would you serve that to your family at home? No. So do you think you can serve it to us? If it's not good enough for your family, are we dogs?' Of course, it was a question of money."

"Every race organizer but the Tour de France itself is always on a limit with the budget, so they called up the hotel and said, 'Look, there's a team coming with eight bike riders and another 10 people or whatever. You've got to feed 18 people, and I'll give you 100 euros for it. So then the hotel goes, 'Okay, I got 100 euros to feed 18 people. That's 10 euros in my pocket because I want to earn money, so I have 90 euros left for 18 people. I'll buy the cheapest meat, the cheapest pasta, and the cheapest sauce."

"So, in the famous French kitchen, the cook couldn't do anything. He had 2.50 Euros per person to feed us. What can you expect? There is no foie gras in the budget – not for 2.50 Euros."

"You can ask anyone from my generation about the race food in French hotels. It was disgusting. Modern riders are lucky in that aspect."

Such stories affect his advice for young hopeful riders. When it comes to food, Jens has some advice for young riders. He says:

"Okay, if you're young, amateur, or a weekend warrior, make it short. Do not overthink it. If you want to race the Tour de France or World Cup races, yes, there will be science involved and calorie counting, and you've got to weigh your body three times a day. But if you just race around the church in your local village, there is no need to go too scientific and spend too much money on healthy food. Stay away from sugary drinks like Cola, Fanta, and all these lemonades. Also, a lot of juices have much more energy than you think. It sounds great as it has vitamin C, yes, but there is a ton of sugar in there. Stay away from chocolate, stay away from too much fatty food, and then you can more or less eat whatever you want. You have the freedom to do it."

Matt Stephens
Pro-rider 1998–2011

STAGE 12

CHICKEN BURRITOS

4 onions
1 garlic clove
1 tsp. sweet paprika
1 can kidney beans
2 limes, juice and zest
1 bell pepper
1 corn cob or small can of corn
1 tsp. ground cumin
1 avocado
400 g cooked chicken
400 g cooked rice
4-8 tortillas
2 tbsp. oil
Fresh coriander
Salt and pepper to taste

1. Peel and slice the onion and garlic. Slice the pepper and cut the corn of the cob.
2. Heat 1 tbsp. oil in a pan and sauté two onions, garlic and paprika until the onions are translucent.
3. Drain half of the water from the canned beans and blend the beans with the soft onion and garlic from the pan. Season to taste with salt and lime juice.
4. Keep the bean purée warm in an extra saucepan over low heat.
5. Wash the pan clean and sauté the rest of the onions with the bell pepper, corn, and cumin. Season to taste with salt and pepper.
6. Halve the avocado and scrape out the flesh. Mash or blend with lime zest and juice. Season to taste with salt and optionally a little freshly grated garlic.
7. Place the bean puree, rice, chicken, and pepper–corn mixture on each tortilla. Fold the tortilla at the sides first and then roll it up and close the bottom.
8. Heat the tortillas on a dry pan before serving. Top with avocado and fresh coriander.

TIP: *Add cheese and jalapeños to the tortilla.*
Replace the chicken with other prepared meat or scrambled eggs.

Easy

 12 pancakes

 3 hours

TORTILLA PANCAKES

(N) (V)

265 g wheat flour
1 tsp. salt
1 tsp. baking soda
40 g butter
150 ml lukewarm water

1. Mix all dry ingredients in a mixer or use a hand mixer with a dough hook.
2. Melt the butter and add it to the flour mixture in a thin stream while the mixer is running. Mix for approx. 30 seconds.
3. Add the water a little at a time and knead the dough well for 2–3 minutes until slightly firm but still wet.
4. Cover the bowl and let the dough rest for 2 hours at room temperature.
5. Divide the dough into 12 equal parts. Form each part into a ball and place on a oven tray lined with baking paper sprinkled with a little flour. Cover and let rest at room temperature for 30 minutes.
6. Sprinkle flour on a flat surface and roll out each dough ball into a pancake of approx. 10 cm./4 inches in diameter. Place each disk on a small piece of baking paper and place another piece of baking paper on top. Repeat with the rest of the the dough balls.
7. Starting from the first disk you rolled out. Roll out the pancakes to a diameter of approx. 20 cm/ 8 inches.
8. Heat up a frying pan, preferably a cast iron pan, over medium-high heat.
9. Fry each pancake on the pan (without oil) for approx. 20–30 seconds on each side.
10. Place the finished pancakes in an airtight container or a plastic bag to steam. Make sure they are covered so that they soften.

TIP: *Eat the pancakes warm or cool.*
You can use the pancakes as wraps for your recovery meal.

THE NEW GRAND TOUR COOKBOOK

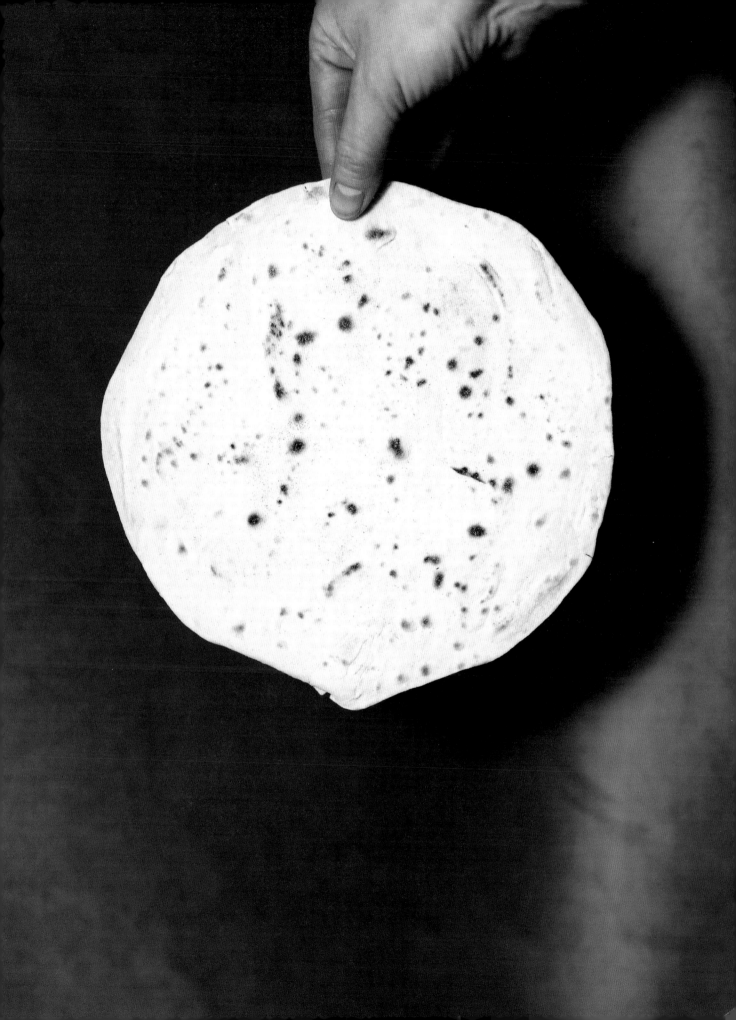

QUESADILLA

100 g cottage cheese
1 egg
50 g cooked beef or chicken
5 pickled jalapeño slices
1 small red onion
Juice of 1 lime
1 tomato
1/2 avocado
1/4 bunch fresh coriander
Salt to taste
2 tortillas

1. Dice the cooked meat and mix it with the cottage cheese, egg, and chopped jalapeño slices. Season with salt and pepper.
2. Finely chop the red onion, tomatoes, and coriander, preferably using a mini chopper. Add the lime juice and avocado and blend into a salsa. Season to taste with salt and pepper.
3. Distribute the cottage cheese filling among the two tortillas and fold them in half.
4. Fry them on a hot pan with a tsp of oil until golden and crispy.
5. Cut them into four parts and serve with the salsa.

TIP: *You can use any kind of leftover meat or fish from the day before.*

STAGE

Easy

 4 people

 10 minutes

AVOCADO AND PEA SALAD *with*

(G) (D) (N) (V) **RASPBERRY VINAIGRETTE**

2 avocados
200 g peas, fresh or frozen
1 cucumber
100 g raspberry
1 pot of pea shoots
Juice of 1 lime
1 butterhead lettuce
1 mini romaine lettuce
2 tbsp. white wine vinegar
1 tbsp. honey
2 tbsp. flavor-neutral oil
Salt and pepper to taste

1. Cut the avocado into slices and season with salt and lime juice.
2. If using frozen peas, place them in cold water and let them thaw for a few minutes.
3. Rinse the cucumber and cut it into slices.
4. Cut off the pea shoots and rinse them if necessary.
5. Mash 5 raspberries with the white wine vinegar and honey. Whisk in the oil and season with salt and pepper.
6. Mix the cucumber, peas, and pea shoots together with 3 tbsp. of the dressing. Season with salt and pepper.
7. Arrange the salad on a plate and top with avocado and fresh raspberries. Serve the rest of the dressing on the side.

TIP: *Serve the salad with cured ham, eggs or cold baked fish and potatoes.*

Easy

 4 burgers

 30 minutes

CORTS *smash* BURGER

200 g mushrooms
2 onions
1 tbsp. balsamic vinegar
400 g minced beef
4 slices cheddar cheese
4 eggs
1 star anise
3 tbsp. olive oil
8 lettuce leaves
4 burger buns
Salt and pepper to taste

TIP: *Yes, you can make a double burger, but as Magnus Cort says: "No, it shouldn't be small burgers or one big one. There should just be a lot of them!" Of course, you can also make your own version of Cort's SMASH burger and give it full gas with mustard, ketchup, mayonnaise, raw onions, pickled cucumbers, and whatever messy ingredients you like.*

1. Cut the mushrooms into thin slices.
2. Peel the onions and cut them finely.
3. Heat up a heavy-bottomed frying pan with 2 tbsp. olive oil and caramelize the onion and mushroom with the star anise over medium-high heat until soft and chewy. Season with salt and balsamic vinegar. Be sure to stir frequently and scrape off any onion that starts to stick to the bottom of the pan so that it doesn't take on a burnt flavor. The onion and mushroom mixture should be soft, caramelized, and delicious. Season the mixture with salt, pepper and balsamic vinegar. Remove the mixture from the pan and keep warm in a bowl.
4. Fry the eggs and keep them warm on a plate under foil while you cook the hamburgers.
5. Form four equal-size balls with the minced beef and heat 1 tbsp. olive oil in a pan, sprinkle with salt.
6. Place two balls of beef in the hot pan and let fry for 30 seconds whilst you grease up a metal spatula with oil.
7. Make smash burgers by pressing the meat balls flat with the spatula. Season with salt and pepper and fry for 1 minute on one side.
8. Turn the hamburgers over and put a slice of cheese on top of each. Cover the pan and fry for 1–2 minutes. The cooking time depends on how flat your hamburgers are and how you want them cooked.
9. Meanwhile, heat the burger buns in the oven. Place the open surface of the buns on the pan after you have removed the hamburgers to soak up the flavor from the pan and to give the buns for a quick caramelization.
10. Assemble the burgers: Bun, lettuce, cucumber, tomato, hamburger patty, onion, and mushroom. Then, spread the egg yolk from a fried egg on the top bun and place the rest of the fried egg on the burger to complete the dish.

FISH BURGER

Fish patty
400 g salmon or tuna fillet
1/2 bunch spring onions
1 tbsp. soy sauce
1 tbsp. fresh ginger
1 tsp. toasted sesame oil
Salt and pepper to taste

Condiments and greens
1 butterhead lettuce
1 avocado
1 mango
1 red onion
Juice of 1 lime
1/4 bunch coriander
1 tbsp. white sesame seeds
2 tbsp. mayonnaise
4 burger buns

1. Dice the fish into small cubes and stir in all of the other burger patty ingredients.
2. Rinse the lettuce and cut the avocado into slices.
3. Dice the mango. Finely mince the red onion and mix it with the mango and a little lime juice.
4. Form four hamburger patties and fry them for about 2 minutes on each side.
5. Heat the burger buns.
6. Build the burger with the mayonnaise, lettuce, hamburger, avocado, mango salsa, sesame seeds, and fresh coriander.

TIP: *Add a little chili powder to the mango salsa.*

Easy

 8 pieces

 2 hours

Ⓓ Ⓝ Ⓥ BURGER BUNS

250 ml lukewarm water

2 tsp. dry yeast

1/2 tbsp. maple syrup

400 g wheat flour
+ plus extra for kneading

1 tsp. salt

2 tbsp. olive oil

1 egg

50 g sesame seeds

1. Dissolve the yeast and maple syrup in the water.
2. Add the wheat flour, salt, and olive oil, knead to form a dough. The dough should be firm and springy.
3. Let the dough rest, covered, for 10 minutes.
4. Sprinkle a little flour on a flat surface and knead the dough until it is smooth and flexible. Place the dough in the mixing bowl and either cover the bowl and leave it in the fridge overnight or cover the bowl and let the dough rise in a warm place for 1 hour until it has doubled in size.
5. Fold the dough, divide it into eight equal pieces, and roll each piece into a burger bun. Press each bun slightly flat, cover with a cloth, and let rise until slightly more than double in size.
6. Preheat the oven to 200°C/390°F.
7. Beat the egg and brush the buns with it. Sprinkle the buns with sesame seeds.
8. Bake for approx. 17 minutes or until they are light brown and sound hollow when tapped on the bottom.

TIP: *These buns are good for sandwiches or breakfast buns.*

Polkadot TIRAMISU

(N) (V)

Biscuit cake layer
2 eggs
55 g sugar
55 g wheat flour

Strawberries and cream
4 pasteurized egg yolks
2 tbsp. sugar + a little extra
1/2 vanilla pod
125 ml whipping cream
200 ml Greek yogurt
20 strawberries
4 tbsp. sweet port wine (optional)

1. Preheat the oven to 190°C/370°F.
2. To make the biscuit layer, beat the eggs with the sugar until white and frothy.
3. Sift the flour and carefully fold it into the egg mass using a rubber spatula.
4. Pour the batter into a greased baking tin sprinkled with flour and bake for approx. 10 minutes or until golden brown. Use a cake tester to test whether the cake is done; there must be no sticky batter on the cake tester. Let it cool down completely.
5. Mash half of the strawberries. Sprinkle sugar and pour the port wine over the strawberry mash.
6. Cut the rest of the strawberries into slices.
7. For the cream, beat the egg yolks with the sugar and vanilla pod until pale yellow and foamy.
8. In another bowl, whip the cream lightly.
9. Fold the egg yolk mixture in with the yogurt. Then, fold that mixture with the lightly whipped cream.
10. Cut the biscuit base crosswise so that you have a layer cake base thickness.
11. Cut 3 appropriately sized circles from the biscuit base to fit your chosen bowl.
12. Layer the cake as follows: biscuit base, strawberry mash, tiramisu cream, and strawberry slices. Repeat until the bowl is full. Make sure the last layer is cream and top with the remaining strawberry slices.
13. Place the tiramisu in the fridge for at least 1 hour (but preferably overnight) before serving.

TIP: *You can use any kind of fruit here.*
Mix 1 tbsp. cocoa powder into the biscuit base and sprinkle chopped chocolate between each cake layer.

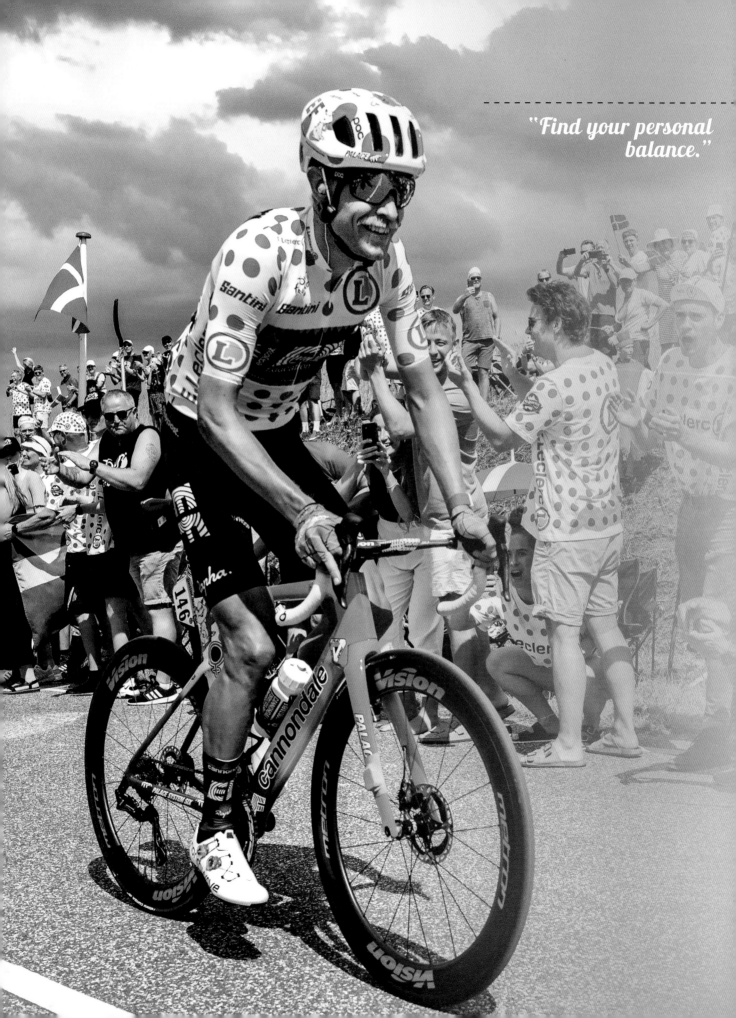

MAGNUS CORT

Pro rider since 2015

Magnus Cort belongs to the generation of riders who were among the first to be nutrition wise. It is the generation that went from years with little or no focus on healthy food and diet to being among the first riders to gain insight and understanding that the right diet is performance enhancing.

From past to present so to speak or so to eat. "I've never counted calories. I still don't, but I've been the first generation to pay attention to getting enough food and not starving yourself," he says.

"In cycling, in the good old days, the philosophy was not to eat much. For many many years as a rider, I simply did not eat enough. At least not at the right times. I rode out and trained and thought the best thing was to drink some mineral water after many kilometers on the roads."

"I think it's because I heard some lectures very early in my career and was a product from the old school of cycling. I heard at those lectures that you should eat during training, after training, and before training. That is when it all began for me, thinking about eating properly and enough. In combination with the fact that I have also never tried to lose weight, I have not been afraid to eat either. Because I haven't needed to lose weight, I have always eaten during training, but most riders did not 15 years ago. It may well be that I eat more today during training than I did then, but back then, I already ate more than many others. I've always had energy drinks in the can, and that was unusual 15 years ago. Today, it is standard."

Certain habits still stick because it works for Magnus Cort. When other riders have different bars and other carbs products in their pockets for training, Cort still has an old-school approach to snacks.

"These are things I can smear with a banana. That is how it has always been for me. As a younger rider, I bought some carb bars a few times, but we didn't have much money, so it was a rare treat. Today, I think I get enough bars when I do bike races, and I am not really a fan, so there are a lot of bananas, bread, and buns on my menu for the long days on the road. It can also be with different types of spreads such as Nutella or Speculoos."

For those who do not know Speculoos, it is a spread made of a very popular Belgian cookie. It suits Magnus Cort, who always chooses sweet things and no other classics such as sandwiches with ham and cheese.

"It must be sweet. Always."

Magnus Cort has worked his way up from the factory floor. From an incomplete education as a bicycle mechanic to riding for small continental teams, he worked his way into the professional universe.

"I moved to Horsens (a Danish town) and lived there for two years in 2013 and 2014. Officially I was not a professional because there I drove for Cult, which is a continental team. But there I rode full time and stopped my education as a bicycle mechanic. I lived like a professional, even though I wasn't officially a professional. We could go out and have lunch in a canteen at a local sponsor company where there was really good food. I almost went to that canteen every day. I finished the workouts there and showed up in my cycling clothes and filled the plate. It was a luxury for a young rider, I tell you that."

During his years as a youth rider, Magnus Cort became more and more aware of the effect of diet. It was a slow and smooth transition from being dependent on the hotel's buffet on race days to driving for teams with their own chefs and nutrition plans.

"Of course, I was in both the junior and U23 national teams, and during the winter, there were various gatherings and lectures, and some of them were also about diet. I have been getting some ideas continuously about what to eat. Among other things, we were in Lanzarote participating in a research and science project, where we were 25 riders and had to live according to a strict diet plan. Actually, because of the diet, I think they had to test something with two different kinds of drinks, but then to make sure we didn't do other weird things that affected the result, we had to eat according to their diet plan."

"It was also interesting to try, and we already had some talks with the researchers so that they could understand us and our nutrition needs but also so that we could understand what could happen. I've been exposed to the effects of a strict diet a bit on a regular basis, but I've never felt like living strictly by weighing my food. I have done it quite a few times. It takes a long time to cook food if you have to weigh each ingredient, and most apps for that purpose can scan barcodes, but if you are in a country without barcodes on food you are in trouble. So I stopped weighing my food and am saving a lot of time."

Yet such attempts and projects have not been a waste of time. Magnus Cort explains that the tests that his generation of riders took part in in the early years provided a basic knowledge that later benefited him: the importance of eating enough, which his generation of riders did not do in the early years. He has taken that understanding with

him but without becoming fanatical about his diet. He explains that he does his usual business.

> *"If I have leftovers from dinner, I will eat them the day after for lunch. I can't stay away from it; it is a habit but it works for me."*

"But I've been pretty good at it; I still am, cooking hot food in the evening. That's the kind of thing I do. I don't really like to cook, and I don't get into it like a foodie, but I feel a hot meal a day is good for me and my inner balance. Breakfast is not difficult. It is oatmeal or porridge. Lunch is also often the same with loaves of bread and a protein shake, and sometimes I make a big smoothie. That is fine for me. I just need some hot food for dinner. It is necessary. In one way or another, I like tasty food, but I am not that keen on investing time in preparing it either. It is a paradox, but I manage to cook my dinner every day no matter [what]."

There is also a difference in Magnus Cort's diet depending on whether he is in- or off-season. This is reflected in what is on the plate.

"I eat several different things when I am away. When I'm at home, it's just one bowl of oatmeal or porridge. Once we are off, there are several options. There are often overnight oats. It is a little different how they are made, or I eat an omelet. I also like two eggs with cheese and ham, which I eat on some bread, and then we often have pancakes. I usually have a snack before I get off the bus, along with a coffee or maybe a waffle with Speculoos. There goes the sweet tooth again."

When the race calendar features the big stage races, with the Tour de France being the biggest and most demanding, the riders' body depots must be thoroughly refueled to match the challenges of the stages. It is a refueling and catering that begins almost as soon as the riders have reached the finish line after exhausting hours on the roads in the French countryside or towering mountains.

"I always drink, and I think most riders do right after the stage, a protein shake. We often get something right at the finish line, which can be a sugary drink of some kind. There might also be sweets, cranberry juice, or something."

"When you cross the finishing line, you are exhausted. And there are a lot of people at the biggest races and stages. You are under pressure on so many aspects, and then you have to focus on drinking so much liquid that you almost can't eat anything later because you get three times half a liter of liquid, like water and sugary drinks, which you have to drink according to the nutrition plan. It is about a balance. It may be that it is actually the carbohydrates that you need the fastest, not the pints of water."

> "I have a philosophy about this part of the big races. It may be smart on paper to get liquid in, which you absorb quickly, but then it is many hours when you don't eat anything solid. You can then go up to seven or eight hours without eating a solid meal, but only drink stuff that gives you energy."

I prefer to have a meal and not just consume sugary drinks. I usually don't wait to eat until we get to the hotel either. I try to eat what I need right after the race in the riders' bus. When we arrive at the hotel, there is usually a food room arranged where you can go in and refuel so that a base has been laid before dinner. A lot of riders do that. However, I usually already eat on the bus on the way to the hotel to get my carbs as fast as possible."

Cycling teams have different strategies for deciding whether or not the riders should eat together. But here too, for Magnus Cort, it's about doing what works best for him and his body after many years of experience.

"Some riders go directly to the food room when we are at the hotel and eat, even if they have already eaten once on the bus. But I do not usually do that. What I instantly need, I eat on the bus en route to the hotel. When we arrive at the hotel, dinner will soon be served anyway. The hotels know dinner must be served rather quickly, as we need to rest and sleep afterward before the next day's stage. For dinner, it can be quite different. Typically, it is rice, pasta, chicken, fish, and cooked vegetables that are prepared for us."

For Magnus Cort, it's about finding the path that works for the individual rider. It is many years of habit, training, and routines that tell him what his body needs to perform. This is also the advice he passes on to young riders.

"Find your balance. Do not train too hard. Find the diets that work for you, but listen to experts and see if there is something that can be used in your everyday life. There is no need to overtrain or be lazy. The most important thing is the long haul, where you find a balance between all the things and you think it's both fun and [that] your body can handle it. You must not drive yourself down one way or the other. The same is true with the daily diet and nutrition. Find your balance."

REST DAY

TOMATOES *and* GREEN BEANS

(G) (V) **WITH FETA CHEESE**

300 g green beans
200 g small tomatoes
1/2 bunch basil
50 g feta
3 tbsp. olive oil
2 tbsp. balsamic vinegar
25 g pine nuts
Salt and pepper to taste

1. Bring a pot of salted water to a boil.
2. Clean the beans and nip off the ends so there are no stems or dry, brown ends.
3. Blanch the beans in the boiling water for 10–15 seconds or until beautifully green but still with a bite. Cool immediately in cold water.
4. Clean and halve the tomatoes. Rinse and pick the basil.
5. Whisk together the olive oil and balsamic vinegar and season with salt and pepper.
6. Toast the pine nuts on a dry pan under supervision over medium heat. Make sure they don't burn.
7. Toss the beans and tomatoes together with the dressing, basil, and crumbled feta. Add salt and pepper to taste. Serve cold for lunch or warm for dinner.

TIP: *You can serve the beans warm if you have everything for the rest of the meal ready when they are done.*
If your olive oil is bitter, you can add a little maple syrup or honey to sweeten it.
Upgrade for lunch: Eat the salad with chickpeas, cooked eggs or chicken.

Easy

 4 people

 20 minutes

CHICKEN SALAD
with APPLE, TARRAGON, AND PICKLED RED ONION

1 red onion

50 ml red wine vinegar

50 ml maple syrup

400 g cooked chicken meat, picked or diced

2 apples

1 celery stalk

25 g pecans or walnuts

200 g Greek yogurt

1 tbsp. Dijon mustard

1 tbsp. honey

1/2 bunch tarragon (or herb of your choice)

2 tbsp. white wine vinegar

Salt and pepper to taste

8 slices sourdough bread, toasted

1. Peel the red onion, cut it into thin slices, and place it in a small bowl.
2. Bring the red wine vinegar and maple syrup to a boil and pour the mixture over the sliced red onions.
3. Dice the apples.
4. Cut the celery into thin slices and chop the pecans.
5. In a bowl, mix the yogurt, Dijon mustard, honey, chopped tarragon, and white wine vinegar together. Season with salt and pepper.
6. Mix the chicken meat with the dressing, apples, celery, and pecans and season with salt and pepper.
7. Arrange the chicken salad on a slice of toasted sourdough bread. Top with pickled onions and another slice of toasted bread.

TIP: *Pickle more onions than you need and use them for delicious topping for sandwiches, wraps or salads.*

Easy 2 people

 10 minutes

SMOKED SALMON
WITH MOZZARELLA, BLUEBERRIES, *and* CRISPY GREENS

300 g romaine lettuce
50 g fresh blueberries
50 ml soy sauce
25 ml maple syrup
1 tbsp. fresh ginger, grated
Zest of 1 organic orange
1 cucumber
1 mozzarella ball
160 g smoked salmon
Toasted sesame seeds

1. Rinse the lettuce and blueberries.
2. In a bowl, mix the soy sauce and maple syrup with the grated ginger and a little finely grated orange zest.
3. Break the lettuce into bite-size pieces and cut the cucumber into long strips. Use a mandolin slicer or a peeler.
4. Break the mozzarella into bite-size pieces
5. Cut the salmon into thin slices.
6. Arrange the lettuce and cucumber on a plate with the salmon and mozzarella and top with the blueberries and dressing.

TIP: *Serve noodles or rice as a side dish.*
Use kale instead of lettuce and cucumber in the winter.
Rinse it and chop it roughly. Mix it together with the dressing before serving.

Medium 6 people

 1 hour and 40 minutes

THOUSAND-LAYER POTATOES

(G) (D) (N) (V)

1.5 kg potatoes
2 onions
2 garlic cloves
50 g grated cheese
(pecorino, parmesan, or gruyere)
2 sprigs fresh thyme (or 2 tsp. dried thyme)
200 ml stock
50 g butter
Salt and pepper to taste

1. Preheat the oven to 200°C/390°F.
2. Peel the potatoes and cut them into 1-2 mm-thick round slices, preferably using a mandolin slicer.
3. Finely mince the onion and garlic.
4. Melt the butter and mix in the potatoes with the onion, garlic, thyme, and cheese, season with salt and pepper.
5. Pour the stock into the bottom of an ovenproof tray and arrange all the potatoes in a nice spiral pattern.
6. Cover the dish with foil, making sure it does not touch the cheese. Bake for 30–40 minutes.
7. Remove the foil and bake for a further 30 minutes or until the potatoes are completely tender. The baking time varies depending on how tightly packed the potatoes are and how thick your ovenproof tray is.
8. Serve hot or cold.

TIP: *You can use all kinds of root vegetables in this recipe. Use what's in season or what you have in your fridge.*
Vary the flavor with different fresh herbs or dried spices, such as smoked paprika, cumin, or garam masala.
You can use whatever cheese you like – it's all delicious.

JUICY, ROASTED CHICKEN *with*

Ⓖ Ⓓ Ⓝ **POTATOES AND ONIONS**

4 red onions
1 kg potatoes
1/2 bunch fresh thyme
1/2 bunch sage
1 chicken (1.3–1.5 kg/ 3lb.)
2 tbsp. oil
Salt and pepper to taste

1. Preheat the oven to 160°C/ 320°F
2. Peel the onions and cut them into quarters.
3. Scrub or peel the potatoes and cut them into bite-size pieces.
4. Rinse the thyme and sage.
5. Mix the onion and potatoes with 1 tbsp. oil and the thyme and sage (save a little sage for the garnish). Season with salt and pepper.
6. Place the onions and potatoes in a braising pan or on an oven-proof tray.
7. Coat the chicken in oil, season it with salt and pepper, and place it on top of the potatoes/onions.
8. Roast for 1 hour.
9. Fry the saved sage leaves until crisp in a little oil on a pan over medium heat, place them on a paper towel, to suck of any excess oil, then season with salt.
10. Let the chicken rest for 10–15 minutes before serving. Top with crisp sage leaves.

TIP: *You can use any type of vegetable under the chicken, just clean out the fridge.*
Also, this dish is so easy and unbelievably juicy and tasty, you can prepare the veggies and chicken in advance and keep it in the fridge and just pop it in the oven 1 hour before you want to eat.
If you roast the chicken in a dutch oven instead of a somewhat flat and open ovenproof tray, you will have more delicious jus left from the chicken to sauce your veggies in.

Easy

 4 people

 20 minutes

OVEN-BAKED
nectarines WITH VANILLA YOGHURT AND CRUMBLE

(G) (N) (V)

4 peaches or nectarines
50 g rolled oats
1/2 tsp. cinnamon
1 tbsp. butter
1 pinch fine salt
200 ml Greek yogurt
1/2 vanilla pod
50 ml + 3 tbsp. maple syrup
Juice of 1 lime

1. Preheat the oven to 185°C/365°F.
2. Halve the nectarines and remove the stones.
3. Pour 2 tbsp. maple syrup on a small ovenproof tray lined with baking paper, sprinkle it with a little fine salt, and place the nectarines on the syrup, cut side down.
4. Bake for approx. 8–10 minutes or until the nectarines are soft but not squishy.
5. Mix the rolled oats with 1 tbsp. maple syrup, butter, and a little bit of fine salt. Toast it golden on a baking sheet in the oven for approx. 10–12 minutes. Turn the sheet halfway through the baking time and stir the mixture a little so that it is baked evenly.
6. Mix the yogurt, vanilla, and 50 ml maple syrup. Season with maple syrup and lime juice.
7. Plate the nectarines and top with vanilla yoghurt and crumble.

TIP: *The baking time is shorter if the fruit is very ripe. You can use any type of stone fruit for this recipe.*
Mix nuts and seeds of your liking into your crumble – and make a lot because it's great tasting as a granola too.

STAGE 16

Easy 4-6 people

 10 minutes

DELICIOUS PINEAPPLE *slaw*
G D V WITH CASHEWS

600 g carrots
1/3 pineapple
1/2 pointed cabbage
50 g cashews
Juice and zest of 1 lime
1 tbsp. maple syrup
2 tbsp. mild olive oil
1/2 tsp. salt
1 tsp. grated ginger

1. Peel the carrots and julienne or grate them roughly.
2. Peel the pineapple and dice it.
3. Cut the pointed cabbage very finely, preferably using a mandolin.
4. Toast the cashews in a dry pan over medium heat until they are nicely golden. Be careful – they burn very quickly. Once toasted, chop them roughly.
5. Mix a dressing from the finely grated lime zest, lime juice, olive oil, salt, and grated ginger.
6. Mix all the ingredients together and top with the toasted cashews.

Medium   4 people

45 minutes

Ⓖ Ⓝ Ⓥ CECILIE'S DHAL

1 large sweet potato
3 onions
1 large piece ginger (25 g)
4 garlic cloves
1 green chili (optional)
200 g tomatoes
30 ml olive oil
1 tsp. ground cumin
1 tsp. mustard seeds
1 tsp. turmeric
1 tsp. ground paprika
Juice and zest of 1 lemon
600 ml water
300 g red lentils
200 g cottage cheese
Fresh coriander
Salt and pepper to taste

1. Preheat the oven to 200°C.
2. Peel the sweet potato and cut it into 2 × 2 cm cubes. Toss the cubes with 1 tbsp. olive oil, season with salt and pepper, and spread them evenly on a piece of baking paper on a baking tray. Bake for approx. 25–30 minutes or until tender and golden brown.
3. Bring the water to boil in a pot and add the lentils. Turn the heat down to medium-low and let simmer for approx. 20–25 minutes or until tender and soft.
4. Peel and finely chop the onion and garlic. Finely chop half of the chili and slice the other half into thin slices. Remove the chili seeds if you don't want it too spicy.
5. Grate the ginger. Cut the tomatoes into bite-size pieces and season with salt and pepper.
6. Heat the remaining olive oil in a saucepan and sauté the onion, garlic, and ginger with the mustard seeds and spices for 5–6 minutes over medium-high heat until completely soft and translucent. Season with salt and pepper.
7. Add the tomatoes and cook for 1 minute.
8. Whisk the onion–tomato mixture into the lentils and season with salt, pepper, and lemon zest and juice.
9. Gently fold half of the sweet potatoes into the lentils.
10. Serve the warm dhal in a deep plate and top with sweet potato, cottage cheese, fresh coriander, and a little fresh chili.

TIP: *Adjust the texture of your dhal with water, some like it more firm, some more soupy.*
If you have smaller sweet potatoes, just scrub them and cut slices instead of dice.

Easy

 4 people

 25 minutes

Delicious ALL ROUND

(G) (D) (N) **MEATBALLS**

Basic meatballs

400 g minced meat of your choice

1 egg

30 g oatmeal/rolled oats

100 ml milk

Salt and pepper to taste

Olive oil

Flavoring

1 large handful mint leaves, chopped

50 g feta, crumbled

Up to 50–75 g other vegetables and spices/herbs

This recipe is great for those nights where you just want dinner done fast. It will work with any type of mince and you can choose the flavor combinations as you like.

1. Preheat the oven to 200°C/390°F.
2. Stir the meatball ingredients together. Add your desired flavorings and season with salt and pepper. Stir the mixture well. Here, you can add a little extra liquid if you want softer and slightly juicier meatballs.
3. Shape golf-ball-size meatballs. If necessary, fry a small meatball in a pan to check whether the seasoning is in order.
4. Place the meatballs on a baking tray lined with baking paper. Sprinkle with olive oil and bake for approx. 6–8 minutes or until the meatballs are firm and beautifully golden brown. You can also fry them in a pan. Here, you must turn them often so that they are fried evenly on all sides.
5. Serve with a side of thinly peeled courgette tossed with lemon juice, olive oil, and salt and pepper.

VARIATIONS: Add fresh herbs, onions, cheese, vegetables, and dried spices. Here are some combinations that I like.

– *Mint and feta*
– *Tarragon, chopped onion, and nutmeg*
– *Parsley and lemon zest*
– *Raisins, pine nuts, and pecorino*
– *Grated cilantro and jalapeños*
– *Cumin, coriander, and smoked paprika*

TIP: *Make a lot! Freeze them in portions, as these all-purpose meatballs are always a lifesaver on a rainy day.*
These meatballs are great cold in sandwiches or salads.

Medium   6 people

90 minutes

APPLE STRUDEL
(N) (V) *in filo*

3 apples
1/2 tsp. cinnamon
1 tbsp. honey
1/2 tsp. salt
1 pack filo pastry
2 tbsp. butter
200 ml Greek yogurt
2 tbsp. maple syrup
1 lemon

1. Peel the apples and cut 2.5 of them into 1 × 1 cm cubes. Mix the cubes with the cinnamon, honey, and salt.
2. Cut the filo pastry into 8 × 24 cm/3 x 9 inch strips. You need 24 strips in total. Save any remaining filo pastry in the freezer.
3. Melt the butter.
4. Place a piece of filo pastry on a cutting board, brush it with butter, and place another piece across it, making a cross.
5. Place another strip of filo pastry perpendicular to the first piece, brush with butter, and lay the last piece across. You now have a filo dough cross with 4 pieces of dough.
6. Place a spoonful of apple mix in the center of the cross and fold the sides into the middle to close the pastry. Place it facing downward on a piece of baking paper. Repeat with the remaining filo pieces.
7. Brush the top of the pastries with butter and put them in the fridge for approx. 30 minutes.
8. Preheat the oven to 190°C.
9. Bake the pastries on a pan for 15–20 minutes or until golden and crispy.
10. Cut the last apple half into thin slices and mix the yogurt with the maple syrup, vanilla, and lemon juice and zest to taste.
11. Serve the warm pastries with yogurt, thin slices of apple, and some finely grated lemon zest.

TIP: *Make these pastries with pear, plum, or pineapple and serve with vanilla ice cream.*
You can make a salty version stuffed with a piece of goat cheese and serve it with apple compote.

'I like the smell of rye
bread in the morning'

CECILIE UTTRUP LUDWIG

Pro rider since 2016

For Cecilie Uttrup, the adventure began as a cyclist in a suburb of Copenhagen when she was a teenager. Back then, she was just looking for a sport that was something for her.

"I grew up in Herlev, close to Copenhagen. I come from a sporty family and have always played sports in one way or another. I've done hundreds of different sports, but nothing really grabbed my attention until the local paper had an article about the local cycling club having its 90th birthday, so they invited people over for a cup of coffee and a hot dog. I thought I have to try that, and I felt really welcomed. Since then, and that was when I was 12 or 13 years old, I have been on a bike. The club lent me a bike at first. If there was something wrong with the bike, I could drop by Monday night for the club night, and they would help. It was just so cool. And then I think I fell in love with cycling – the thing about going out and then just getting the wind in your hair, meeting friendly people, and feeling welcome. So, it kind of developed from there."

As a child in a sporty family, healthy food and lots of greens were served, so thoughts about food and diet were not new to her.

"No, I grew up eating healthy. And ate lots of vegetables. When you're little and growing up, you think it's cool to eat something that's unhealthy, but I came from a home where everybody ate rye bread in the morning. And there was plenty of fruit. My mother always made packed lunches. And I remember the others in class being so

jealous. The others sat and looked over at my packed lunches and wanted me to share the packed lunch. It was just normal for me to eat solid and healthy food."

"And when I had friends over, my mother always came up and knocked on the door. You always think it is so embarrassing: 'Yes, mother, what do you want now?' Then, she always came in with snacks. As in apples, carrots, and peppers. She always came in with something like that. And my friends thought it was so cool. They were just like, 'oh yeah, fruit man.' And I just think it was so embarrassing: 'Mom, can't you bring candy?' It was so funny."

From an early age, she understood there were no easy solutions when it came to training regarding sugar, light carbohydrates, or other easy options. The healthy packed lunches also proved successful when Cecilie was looking after her training as a teenager.

"I always grew up with rye bread in the morning. The smell of rye bread in the morning is so memory lane. I love it. And you know, with various kinds of toppings. I also loved that there were some cold cuts and such. Then, [there's] the thing about eating rye bread with cold cuts when you are actually training and going fast. The others ate bars. I had my rye bread. People thought it was weird."

The Danish world-famous rye bread has followed her ever since, from her teenage years to her time as a professional.

"I'm a rye bread girl. I love rye bread so much. And I miss it when I am here in Spain. So, rye bread is for me. It is the taste of Denmark. It is so good. I love rye bread and buns too. But it was very important to my mother that they were solid and healthy buns. We always made sure I got a lot of chicken. And actually, also throughout my upbringing, there was really a lot of chicken, a lot of rice, and a lot of pasta – so many of the things that I actually eat now too. And gravy. I really love gravy."

Cecilie Uttrup's mother was very focused on her daughter's diet and nutrition. Cecilie took that with her when she became a professional rider.

"When I was around 20 years old, I was paid to be a cyclist. It is a bit of an adventure and a privilege, but I did not forget my eating habits from back home."

Her meeting with the professional world was also a meeting with a universe that cared a lot about the right diet and nutrition.

"The teams didn't have a nutritionist, but they paid a lot of attention to food. But for me, it wasn't anything hugely new because I think, actually, that because I come from a home where we've been quite focused on healthy food and because I've always been quite interested in diet myself, it wasn't mind-blowing for me. But it's true, it gradually became more professional. But I think it only became really professional when I ended up on the race team Française des Jeux. It is my fourth year now. We have also got a food truck now on the team. Not many women's teams have that. But everyone goes more into it now and down to the little details."

It is possible to get an individual diet plan, but Cecilie Uttrup has opted out. She chooses to listen to her body and instead focuses on training and performance without devoting too much time to her diet.

"Personally, I don't have a diet plan. But if I ask, I can get it. I think if you had a very strict diet plan, you have to eat this and this, and you have to weigh your food. I mean someone does that and weighs throughout the day what they eat. I think I would get too focused on it. I think I generally have a pretty good understanding of what my body needs."

As long as the rider stays within a weight limit and rides well, then there is the freedom to choose her own diet, but Cecilie also receives feedback from her team management through entries about her food intake. This means she can adjust her daily diet as needed.

"During races, it is important that we fuel correctly when we are on the bike. We report what we eat along the way, and the data are used for analyzing if we need something for the next day. As I said, I am not super strict on it, but it is really a help with this kind of feedback. If we are in deficit, then we are told that we must eat x number of grams of pasta in the evening. I think that is cool. That is insanely cool."

"There are some riders who burn an awful lot, and some don't burn as much, or less. In this way, the guideline that we get is that you should eat 100 grams of carbohydrates per hour.

"If it is, for example, the Tour de France, then you are also told that before that climb, you must remember to eat like this. Or remember to eat something at the top of the climb so you don't sit at the bottom and completely lack energy."

For the big races, including the classics and stage races like the Grand Tours, Cecilie follows her own set routine that begins at breakfast.

"The stages usually start around 12. Then, I like to eat three hours before riding out. I eat yogurt, oatmeal, muesli, and stuff like that in the morning. And then, depending on if the start is a little later, I eat a little again. But not a big meal.

I like to eat an omelet or a few eggs in the morning. And then I feel full longer. And yes, during the stage, we will, as I said, know if more needs to be consumed. And then I just drive."

Most riders have a sweet tooth and have bars and other sweet energy cakes in their pockets to eat during the stages to keep their energy up when the body's stores are running low. It is no different for Cecilie Uttrup. She is a cake lady, she says.

"That is those energy cakes. They taste good. They are delicious. Or rice cakes with assorted flavors. It's always delicious to have a small snack. So yes, I crave cake and sugar when we are in-season and sweets, and I eat a lot of energy wine gums."

After the stages, there is a need to fill up not only with sugar and energy, but fuel up for the following day. There is a large selection of meal options waiting in the riders' bus.

"Sometimes it's sandwiches. Other times it's pasta, rice, gnocchi, and then it's some meat. It can be chicken. And then a salad. It's all good, but the favorite when I get on the bus is a bag of sweets or an ice cream. It is my guilty pleasure."

Once at the riders' hotel, the riders either refuel from the hotel's buffet or the team's own food truck, where the bike team's chef has prepared plates for them.

"You can easily take more if you want. But what is on the plate, that's the minimum. You must eat that. I love gnocchi, and then I love sweet potatoes like that. Avocado is necessary, and I like fish when it comes to protein. A salmon that is well cooked is delicious. Dessert can be a chocolate mousse made from protein powder, but not all riders like these kinds of tricks. It must be the food it looks like not powder magic."

Food must be effective and taste good at the same time because it is a morale booster. In addition to getting eight to nine hours of sleep, Cecilie Uttrup will advise young riders to think about their diet.

"It means a lot to be fueled correctly - that you eat enough when you bike out and get the carb load right. You don't want to go broke on carbs. It is hell."

"It is difficult to give advice in general because it is often the case that if I met a young girl, I would give her one kind of advice, and if I met a slightly older gentleman, I would give another [piece of] advice. Then I would say, for example to a young girl, I really want to emphasize that eating should be fun and not a duty or a strict plan, which can be a misunderstood expression of self-control in the teenage years. Food and meals should not be about that. The diet gives us energy on the bike and for training, and it is important that you think about what you eat but also allow yourself to have fun. It can be good for morale to appreciate your food so much that you look forward to the next meal. It can mean a lot during the hard times on the bike to think about a hot meal waiting at the end of the stage."

"Food is your friend and you should enjoy that friendship."

STAGE 17

Easy   2-4 people

 45-50 min

CRISPY *smashed* POTATOES

(G) (D) (N) (V)

400 g potatoes with skin
Olive oil
Salt and pepper to taste

1. Preheat the oven to 200°C / 395°F.
2. Boil the potatoes in unsalted water until they are completely soft.
3. Pour olive oil on a baking tray. Use baking paper instead if you know the potatoes will stick to the tray.
4. Place the potatoes on the tray and press them flat with a flat bottom cup or metal spatula.
5. Season with salt and pepper and drizzle with olive oil.
6. Roast in the oven for approx. 25–30 minutes or until completely crispy and golden.
7. Serve with dip as a side for a chicken, beef, fish, or burger.

TIP: *You can season the potatoes with dried spices or herbs, such as smoked paprika, chili, cumin, dried oregano, or rosemary.*

REMEMBER: *The baking time depends on the water content of the potatoes and how flat they are pressed. Use potatoes with a high starch content (old potatoes) to get the nicest, flattest potatoes. The longer you bake them, the crispier they get.*

Easy

 4 people

 20 minutes

TOMATOES *with* DEVILED EGGS

(G) (N) (V)

4 eggs [M/L]
300 g tomatoes of different colors
1 tsp. capers
4–5 cornichons
1/2 tsp. Dijon mustard
1/2 tbsp. Greek yogurt
4 spring onions
1 tbsp. olive oil
1/4 bunch dill, chopped
Salt and pepper to taste

1. Bring water to a boil in a saucepan. Spoon in the eggs, set a timer, and hard-boil the eggs for approx. 9 minutes. If your eggs are very large, the cooking time will be longer; if they are very small, the cooking time will be shorter – check out the egg guide in the book.
2. Once cooked, cool the eggs down immediately in cold water.
3. Cut the tomatoes into slices and season them with salt and pepper. Finely chop the spring onions.
4. Peel and halve the eggs and gently remove the yolks.
5. Chop the capers and cornichons and blend them with the boiled egg yolks, 1 tbsp. spring onion, Dijon mustard, and yogurt. Season to taste with salt and pepper.
6. Spoon the egg yolk filling back into the boiled egg white halves.
7. Arrange the tomatoes on a plate with the eggs and top with the remaining spring onions, dill, and olive oil.

TIP: *You can use any type of fresh herbs or dried spices and add chili for a nice spicy kick.*

Medium 4 people

90 minutes

COQ au VIN BLANC

1 whole chicken or 4 large chicken thighs
2 tbsp. olive oil
4 leeks
1 fennel bulb
3 onions
1 whole head of garlic
500 ml white wine
500 ml chicken stock
1 tbsp. honey
2 tbsp. white wine vinegar
4 rosemary stalks
2 star anise
1/2 tsp. black peppercorns
1 tsp. coriander seeds
4 bay leaves
1 bunch fresh parsley
Juice and zest of 1 lemon
Salt and pepper to taste
300 g brown rice

1. Preheat the oven to 170°C/340°F.
2. Divide the chicken into eight parts: upper thigh, drumstick, breast, and wings. If you use whole thighs, they must be divided at the joint into the upper and lower thighs. Season with salt and pepper. Flip the pieces in flour if you want the sauce to thicken a little.
3. Brown the chicken pieces in dutch oven or frying pan over medium-high heat. If using a frying pan, transfer the pieces to a large ovenproof dish once browned.
4. Cut the leeks into thin rings. Clean the rings in a large bowl of water and lift them out of the water, so that any sand or dirt stays in the bottom of the bowl.
5. Peel the onions and cut them into quarters. Rinse the fennel and cut it into 6–8 wedges.
6. Brown the onion and fennel in olive oil over high heat in a pan and then spread them around the chicken together with the leeks.
7. Fill a tea bag with the peppercorn, coriander seeds, and star anise and place it next to the chicken along with the bay leaves.
8. Add the stock, honey, vinegar, and rosemary to the dish. Season with salt and pepper. Make sure that the skin of the chicken is just above the liquid's surface, like the tip of an iceberg.
9. Bake for approx. 1 hour or until the chicken is completely tender and cooked through.
10. Pick the parsley.
11. Whilst the chicken is in the oven, cook the rice according to the instructions on the bag.
12. Season the dish with salt, pepper, and a little lemon juice.
13. Serve topped with fresh parsley and lemon zest alongside the cooked rice.

TIP: *You can add any types of vegetables and fresh herbs that are in season.*
You can thicken the sauce with 2–3 tbsp. flour beaten together with a little water. Bring the sauce to a boil before you taste and season it again.

Easy

 4 people

 30 minutes

PASTA ROMESCO

400 g pasta
2 red bell peppers
2 garlic cloves
50 g roasted almonds
100 ml olive oil
1 tsp. smoked paprika
30 ml water
40 g pecorino or parmesan
2–3 tbsp. red wine vinegar
Ground black pepper and salt

1. Cut the bell peppers into rough cubes.
2. Peel and finely chop the garlic.
3. Heat a little olive oil in a frying pan. Fry the bell peppers over high heat until they are cooked through and take on a nice, dark color.
4. Lower the heat, add the garlic, and sauté for 1 minute.
5. Blend the cooled bell pepper mixture with the remaining ingredients, except for the water and pasta. Adjust the texture with a little water until you have a smooth pesto.
6. Season to taste with salt, vinegar, and a little cayenne pepper (optional).
7. Bring a large pot of salted water to a boil.
8. Cook the pasta according to the instructions on the bag. Once al dente, toss it with the pesto.
9. Serve topped with freshly grated parmesan or pecorino.

TIP: *The Romesco sauce is great for sandwiches, salads and wraps too.*

STAGE 18

Easy

 4 people

 25-30 minutes

RICE, RICE BABY

100 g rice
150 ml water
1/2 tsp. salt
1 bunch parsley
50 g toasted almonds
Juice and zest of 1 lemon

TIP: *You can toast the rice in a little olive oil at the bottom of the pan before adding the water for a nuttier taste. You can also cook the rice in stock.*

For a rider, rice on the menu every day can easily get bit boring. Here are suggestions for how to make your daily portion of rice more fun. For all recipes, cook the rice first.

1. Bring the water and rice to a boil.
2. Turn down the heat and let simmer for 10–12 minutes until all water is absorbed.
3. Leave the rice to finish steaming with the lid on for 10–12 minutes.
4. Pick the parsley. Pour boiling water over it and then squeeze out the liquid.
5. Roughly chop the parsley and blend with a little water to make a thick puree.
6. Chop the toasted almonds.
7. Mix the rice and parsley puree together. Season with lemon zest and juice, salt, and pepper. Arrange on a platter topped with toasted almonds.

Here are some other ideas of what you can do with rice:
Rice pilau: Sauté sliced onion in a little olive oil until tender. Add the rice and sauté for approx. 1 minute. Add water and cook according to the instructions. You can also add turmeric to the onions.

Coriander–lime rice: Cook the rice according to the instructions. Then, stir in finely chopped fresh coriander and lime zest and juice. You can also add coconut flour (preferably toasted).

Coconut rice: Rinse the rice well and cook it according to the instructions, replacing half the water with coconut milk.

Cinnamon and almond rice: Cook the rice with 1 cinnamon stick, 1 star anise, and 4–5 cardamom capsules. Remove the whole spices once the rice has cooked. Mix the rice with toasted almonds.

Turmeric, cinnamon, and cumin rice with raisins and chickpeas: Cook the rice according to the instructions. Heat olive oil in a pan and sauté the raisins, spices, and cooked chickpeas. Toss the rice with the mixture.

FALAFEL WAFFLE *with*
SALTED RED CABBAGE, POMEGRANATE AND YOGURT DRESSING

(G) (N) (V)

Falafel
400 g dried chickpeas (not canned)
1/2 tsp. baking soda
1 small bunch fresh parsley, stems removed
1 bunch fresh coriander
1/2 bunch dill
1 small onion
4 garlic cloves
Salt to taste
1 tbsp. ground black pepper
1 tbsp. ground cumin
1 tbsp. ground coriander
1 tsp. cayenne pepper (optional)
1 tsp. baking soda
2 tbsp. toasted sesame seeds
Rapeseed oil for frying (not cold-pressed)

Cabbage and dressing
1/4–1/2 head red cabbage
1 pomegranate
250 ml yogurt
Juice and zest of 1 lemon
1 bunch fresh mint, chopped
Salt and pepper to taste

1. Soak the chickpeas in cold water for at least 12 hours (preferably 24 hours). Change the water every 12 hours.
2. Strain the chickpeas and blend all ingredients, except for the baking powder and sesame seeds, in a food processor until it has a wet granulated texture, approx. 1 minute, you should be able to easily form little balls out of it without it falling a part. Season to taste with salt.
3. Leave the falafel mix in the fridge for at least 1 hour or overnight before frying.
4. Just before frying, mix the baking powder and sesame seeds into the mix.
5. Heat up your waffle maker, brush with olive oil, and fill with a large spoonful of falafel mix. Bake the waffle for 5–6 minutes or until it is golden brown and cooked through. Continue with the remaining mix.
6. Cut the red cabbage very finely and massage it for 1 minute with a little fine salt until soft.
7. Halve the pomegranates and knock out the pomegranate seeds into a bowl with paper towels.
8. Mix the yogurt with the lemon zest and chopped mint and season with salt and pepper.
9. Serve the falafel waffle topped with red cabbage, pomegranate seeds, yogurt dressing and fresh mint.

TIP: *You can also shape the falafel into "hamburger patties" or small ball and fry them on a pan if you don't have a waffle maker.*
Freeze any leftover cooked falafels and just re-heat them in the oven.

KOFTA *with* COURGETTE AND QUINOA

Köfte

1 red onion
200 g minced lamb
200 g minced beef
1/2 squash
4 garlic cloves
1/2 bunch parsley
2 tsp. ground coriander
1 tbsp. ground cumin
1/4 tsp. cayenne pepper
1/4 tsp. allspice
1 tsp. ground cinnamon
1/2 tsp. ground ginger
Salt and pepper to taste
8 wooden or metal skewers

Tabouleh

300 g quinoa
1/2 bunch coriander
100 g small tomatoes
1 red onion
1 lemon
3 tbsp. olive oil
Salt and pepper to taste

1. Peel the red onion, cut 1 it into rough cubes, and mince it in a mini chopper or with a stick blender until it is completely pureed. Squeeze out all of the liquid with your hands and place the onion puree in a bowl. Mince the other onion for the taboule and marinate in lemon juice in a bowl.
2. Finely grate the courgette and garlic and chop the parsley.
3. Stir the rest of the köfte ingredients together with the onion and season well with salt and pepper. Knead for 2–3 minutes.
4. Divide the mix into 8 equal parts and shape into oblong meatballs around each skewer. Let rest for 1 minute, 1 hour, or, preferably, a few hours – however if you're starving – just cook them straight away.
5. If you use wooden skewers, soak them in cold water for a few minutes so that there are no splinters in the meat.
6. Heat the oven to 200°C/390°F and bake the köfte skewers for 10–12 minutes or until they are firm and cooked through.
7. Cook the quinoa according to the instructions on the bag.
8. Pick the coriander. Cut the tomatoes into bite-size pieces and season with salt and pepper. Mix the quinoa with tomato, miced onion, olive oil, lemon zest and seaso with salt and pepper.
9. Serve the köfte on the tabouleh.

TIP: *You can go with just beef if you are not a lamb person.*
Serve with couscous, bulgur, or similar.
Serve the yogurt dressing from the falafel waffle recipe with the kofta.

RASPBERRIES WITH LEMON CURD
 AND *crispy* **FILO PASTRY**

1 pack filo pastry
12 pitted medjool dates
1 lemon, juice and zest
50 ml boiling water
6 tbsp. melted butter
1 pinch salt
1 tray raspberries
200 ml yogurt
2 tbsp. maple syrup
1/2 vanilla pod

1. Preheat the oven to 170°C/335°F.
2. Melt the butter over low heat.
3. Cut the filo pastry into strips approx. 10 cm wide, place them on a baking tray lined with baking paper and bake them for 8–10 minutes or until crispy and golden.
4. Soak the dates in boiling water for 5 minutes.
5. Blend the dates with the water, lemon zest and juice, and salt into a puree, start with half of the water and add more if needed – if your lemons are huge, you might not need all of it.
6. Add the melted butter into the mixture little by little, blend until smooth, and season with salt to taste.
7. Mix the yogurt with the vanilla and maple syrup.
8. Arrange the lemon curd with the yogurt, crispy filo, and raspberries on a plate.

TIP: *Brush he filo with a bit of melted butter and sprinkle nuts or a bit of sugar on it.*

STAGE 18

Easy · 2-4 people · 40 minutes

SHEETPAN RATATOUILLE with CHICKPEAS

G D N V

2 red onions
2 garlic cloves
2 courgette
1 eggplant
2 red peppers
200 g small tomatoes
2 rosemary stalks
3 tbsp. balsamic vinegar
1 bunch basil
Juice and zest of 1 lemon
400 g cooked / canned chickpeas
Salt and pepper to taste

1. Preheat the oven to 185°C/365°F.
2. Peel the onion and garlic. Slice the onion into strips and finely chop the garlic.
3. Dice the courgette and eggplant into approx. 2 × 2 cm dice.
4. Pierce the tomatoes with a sharp knife.
5. Pick and chop the rosemary.
6. Mix all the greens together with the chickpeas, olive oil, rosemary, and balsamic vinegar and season with salt and pepper.
7. Roast everything in the oven on a baking sheet with baking paper for 20–25 minutes or until tender and golden.
8. Mix in the picked basil and season with finely grated lemon zest and juice, salt, and pepper.

TIP: *Serve this dish hot or cold. You can serve rice on the side. Add chiffonade pointed cabbage to any cold leftovers for a delicious salad.*

STAGE 19

TUNA- AND EGG SALAD *with* PEAR

(G) (N)

2 cans good-quality tuna in water

4 hard-boiled eggs

1/2 bunch dill

1/2 bunch chives

1 lemon

200 ml Greek yogurt

1 tsp. Dijon mustard

1 large red onion

2 bulbs

100 ml white wine vinegar

4 tbsp. maple syrup

10-12 blackberries

Salt and pepper to taste

Sometimes, a meal just needs to be simple and relaxed, and a good tuna salad is always a hit at lunch time. It works for sandwiches, salads, and wraps after a workout.

1. Boil a pot of water and add the eggs once the water boils. Boil for 10 minutes, and immediately shock in cold water.
2. Peel and mince the onion and put it in a small bowl.
3. Bring the vinegar and maple syrup to a boil and pour it over the onion.
4. Drain the water from the tuna and place the tuna meat in another bowl.
5. Peel and chop them roughly and toss them with the tuna, Greek yogurt, and Dijon mustard.
6. Finely chop the herbs – save some for the garnish.
7. Quarter the cored pears and then dice them into small dice.
8. Stir the tuna and egg salad together with the herbs, drained pickled onions and pears.
9. Season with lemon zest and juice, salt, and pepper.
10. Top with blackberries and serve as a salad.

Medium 4 people

 1 hour and 30 minutes

MADS P's LASAGNA

Bolognese
400 g minced beef
4 carrots
2 onions
3 celery stalks
3 garlic cloves
300 ml red wine
1 tbsp. dried basil
2 tsp. dried oregano
1 tsp. dried thyme
4 bay leaves
80 g tomato puree
2 cans chopped tomatoes
400 ml stock
1 star anise
Salt and pepper to taste
Olive oil

Bechamel
1 L milk
100 g flour
100 g butter
Grated nutmeg to taste
Salt and pepper to taste

100 g grated mozzarella
100 g grated parmesan
1 package lasagna sheets

Bolognese:
1. Brown the minced beef well in a large pan with a little olive oil. Season with salt and pepper.
2. Peel the carrots, onion, and garlic and clean the celery. Now, you can either cut all of the vegetables into rough pieces and finely chop them into granules in a food processor or grate the carrots and finely chop the onion, garlic, and celery.
3. Add 2–3 tbsp. olive oil to the pan and sauté all the greens until tender and soft over medium heat together with the dried herbs.
4. Add the tomato puree and stir.
5. Turn up the heat to medium-high, pour in red wine, bring it to a boil and let it reduce down to 1/3 of its original volume.
6. Add the tomatoes and stock and bring to a boil while stirring. Lower the heat and let simmer for 15–20 minutes.
7. Preheat the oven to 170°C/340°F

Béchamel:
8. Boil 200 ml of water in a kettle and warm up the milk.
9. Melt the butter in a saucepan over medium heat and stir in the flour until you have a paste. Let it cook while stirring constantly for 1–2 minutes.
10. Add the boiling water to the paste and whisk until the flour mixture has dissolved. Add the milk a little at a time while whisking and let it boil each time.
11. Let the sauce gently boil over low-medium heat while stirring constantly so that the sauce does not burn.
12. Add grated parmesan and stir until melted into the sauce. Season with grated nutmeg, salt, and pepper.
13. Take a large ovenproof tray and cover the bottom with a layer of bechamel. Place a layer of lasagna sheets down, then a layer of Bolognese sauce, and then a layer of bechamel. Repeat until you have used all ingredients. The last layer must be bechamel.
14. Top with grated mozzarella and bake for 45–60 minutes.
15. Cover and let rest for at least min. 15 minutes before serving so that it does not lose its form.

MADS *P's* PANCAKES

(N) (V)

3 eggs
250 ml milk or plant milk
3 tbsp. maple syrup
50 g butter
100 g wheat flour
1 pinch fine salt
1 tsp. cardamom
Zest of 1 lemon
Fresh berries

1. Whisk the eggs, milk, and sugar together.
2. Sift the wheat flour into a bowl and mix it with the cardamom and salt.
3. Whisk the egg mass into the flour mixture and add the grated lemon peel.
4. Melt the butter and whisk it into the dough in a thin stream.
5. Let the dough rest for 10 minutes.
6. Melt a little butter in a pan over medium-high heat and pour approx. 50 ml of batter into the pan. Spread it quickly by tipping the pan around.
7. Fry the pancakes until golden brown on both sides. Keep the pancakes warm on a plate covered with foil as you finish baking the rest of them.
8. Serve with fresh berries.

TIP: *Make it festive - serve the pancakes with ice cream.*
Pancakes are great for bringing on rides. Roll them up with hone, jam or one of the date pastes from the book.

"Find your way."

MADS PEDERSEN

Pro rider since 2017

Mads Petersen has been a professional rider for six years, but it was not always in the cards for him to choose cycling as a way of life. It was a soccer coach who sent him in that direction because Mads was a bad loser and had a temper not suited for team sports!

"I played soccer like everyone else, but quickly the coach told my parents that maybe I should find something else to do. I had a fiery temper and was a bad loser. My father only used to cycle for exercise, and then I saw him cycling and asked if I could get a bicycle too. Then he found some old piece of junk with two wheels that I could ride a bit on, and I have been on the bike ever since I was seven years old. Cycling was more me than soccer. I even participated in races before I was old enough."

As a child in a family where sport played a big role, there was always food on the table dedicated to a diet that suited active children with a hectic sporting life. It was traditional food, but with considerations for saving time while serving good, healthy food.

"My mother is a nurse and knows well how to 'fuel' the body, so it has always been considered. But with three boys in the house, there has never been much time to cook either. I have two brothers both playing soccer. We have always lived healthily, as we should, but with shortcuts. There have been easy solutions due to time pressure, but healthy food was always served throughout. We really had to make an effort about getting a pizza, let me put it that way."

As a teenager, he started helping around the house and learned to prepare various pasta dishes, but the diet did not fill much for the aspiring rider, who is not afraid to admit to a guilty pleasure.

"If you read my book, it appears that I didn't think too much about if I ate a little too much and was too heavy. I now know that diet matters a lot. It is important to be proper with things. So, you can be an athlete and have a good relationship with food. And you can have your desires satisfied if you have a sweet tooth like I do who wants everything sugary. I know it's totally wrong what's coming here, but I love a burger from McDonald's too. It's really good, but I could satisfy the urge in a significantly healthier way by getting to know things myself, so over time I learned a lot just by listening to my body."

When Mads Petersen is off-season, he manages his diet planning to achieve a small weight loss. He is not a fanatic but has found his own way to manage his diet by reducing his food intake during the day and consuming a lot of carbohydrates during his long training hours.

"It's about finding a balance about how much you can cut without it affecting the training. And I've found that if I run really heavy on carbs during training, I can actually eat less for the rest of the day and then still get the right output from my training sessions. I eat a mix of proteins with a little bit of carbs in the morning – that is toast with eggs and some ham. And only two slices because toast bread goes in and works immediately with your body depots. I have to train an hour later, so there is instant energy. The protein helps to repair and also provides some energy. During training, I eat 100 to 120 carbs per hour."

During that time of year, he refrains from consuming carbohydrates for dinner. To control his weight loss and if a snack is needed, he consumes a protein yogurt.

"If I can feel that in the three hours between my last meal and dinner I need something more, then I take a protein yogurt. There are 150 calories in one, and you get 30 grams of protein, and then the body has something more to repair and work with. And for dinner, I actually avoid carbohydrates when I want to lose weight. So, it's really just protein and vegetables on my plate."

This goes against the typical recommendations during the training period, as it is normal to think of consuming carbohydrates at dinnertime. But Mads Petersen does it his own way because it works for him.

"That is just the way I've made it work. I can see the weight coming off quickly. Because I still have my training working 100% as it should, because I have the huge intake of carbs during the training, I am not missing anything."

> "*As soon as we drive off the starting block, I eat something almost from the first second - some kind of carbs, the equivalent of two regular potatoes, maybe. These are the carbohydrates that I eat.*"

"Regarding protein, it's usually a really big piece of chicken, like 350 grams, relatively much, and then vegetables for the rest of my meals. For God's sake, you must not sit and feel overfed. [There's] nothing worse than feeling heavy. There's no reason for that. If you want to lose weight, then stop eating when you are not feeling hungry. Then, the weight loss will come fast."

When the season is underway with a break between races, typically in the spring, Mads Pe-tersen takes a different approach to his nutrition. There are similarities with the off-season, but also differences, where potatoes, in particular, play a role.

"I actually stay away from classics like oatmeal. The thing about eating oatmeal, it's typically our parents' thing. They say, now you just must fill up, oatmeal is a good base, and you're ready. But oatmeal works three hours after breakfast because it still takes some time for the body to get the oatmeal going."

"If I eat a huge batch of oatmeal and go out and train 45 minutes later, I have no energy, nutri-tionally speaking, unless I eat something that is quickly absorbed during training and before we're two hours into training. I mainly just eat something that is relatively light and without any particularly good energy in it, but it gives a base straight from when I start, and then I'm up there on the right track from the training side. I pretty much do that all year round. But then lunch will be a bit different because there I eat a bit more carbohydrates. I pretty much cut out the vege-tables for lunch; it's just about getting protein, whether it's with beans or eggs or meat or whatever the hell it is – it doesn't really matter. It is just protein and then carbs. Proper fuel. I love pasta – it tastes insanely good – but my stomach works better with potatoes or rice. I usually stick to one of the two things. And then for dinner, half of my dinner should be vegetables and then carbohydrates and a little meat for the rest. Very little meat."

However, it is not just potatoes and rice that are served. Mads Petersen has a craving that is a bit special in relation to cycling races. Yes, pancakes.

"I don't even know if you can call it decent food. I discuss that with my wife every time. I tell her, pancakes, I love pancakes, and I can easily eat pancakes with ice cream for dinner. I just love it, and like when we do bike races, I am allowed to have it for breakfast, just not the ice cream. But I can have pancakes. Thank God."

This does not mean that Mads Petersen will have a big tower of pancakes on a plate waiting for him in the riders' bus after the races. It is a completely different, pragmatic serving that awaits after the races when athletes need to refuel quickly after a long day eating miles.

"There is always some chicken salad, and then there is typically the classic white rice. Potatoes can also be there sometimes and omelets. It must be carbohydrates and the opportunity to fill up on proteins."

Although it requires a special diet to be a professional cyclist, Mads Petersen wants to encourage young riders to relax about it and not become fanatical. It is about maintaining the joy of cycling and the motivation to get out on the country roads, rather than letting a killer diet dictate your life.

"If it's a 13- to 14-year-old beginner, I would never ever tell them that they should eat at specific times and only this and this much. You are also in the growing age at that time. If you eat right and exercise, you can hardly eat too much. But I think at that age, I would tell them at least to remember to drink a lot of water. And then you have to try to eat healthily."

"'Now stop drinking a Coke every day, even if it's sugar-free and all sorts of crap. Just drink water, drink water, drink water, and then try to cut out all that fake sugary crap."

This does not mean that young riders and their parents should be completely scared of sugar. It's just about using your common sense when it comes to one's diet.

"If you eat a proper biscuit once in a while, that's not what makes the difference at that age at all. If it's candy, that's just not healthy for your body. And you can tell pretty quickly that you don't do those things. This means young riders should eat as much as they like but go very easy on the soft drinks and sweets. And if it's the middle-aged amateur rider who wants to up his or her game, try cutting out the alcohol. Going from one glass every day to three glasses of wine a month is a big step in the right direction. Drink water instead."

STAGE

Easy

 2-4 people

 15 minutes

BRUSCHETTA
with TOMATO, FETA AND OREGANO

(N) (V)

4 bread slices
200 g small tomatoes
3 tbsp. balsamic vinegar
1 tbsp. honey
50 g feta cheese
Fresh oregano
2 tbsp. olive oil
Salt and pepper to taste

1. Preheat the oven to 200°C/390°F.
2. Cut the tomatoes into bite-size cubes and toss with balsamic vinegar and honey. Season with salt and pepper.
3. Place the four slices of bread on a baking tray lined with baking paper. Spread the tomatoes on the bread and top with crumbled feta. Drizzle with olive oil and season with salt and pepper.
4. Bake for approx. 8–10 minutes and finish with a broil. Make sure it doesn't burn.
5. Serve warm topped with fresh oregano.

TIP: *You can replace the feta with another cheese according to your taste.*
You can also use gluten-free bread.

DOUBLE BAKED
(G) (N) (V) *jacket* POTATOES

4 large baking potatoes
200 ml yogurt
1/2 bunch dill
1/2 bunch chives
Juice and zest of 1 lemon
1 tsp. Dijon mustard
2 tbsp. olive oil
Salt and pepper to taste
50 g parmesan
1/2 bunch chervil (French parsley)

1. Preheat the oven to 200°C/390°F.
2. Wrap the baking potatoes in foil and bake for 45–60 minutes or until completely tender. Let cool.
3. Rinse and chop 2/3 of the dill and chives.
4. Cut the top off the potatoes and scrape out the insides. Make sure the potato skins don't fall apart.
5. Stir the potato insides with the chopped herbs, 2/3 of the yogurt, lemon zest and juice, Dijon mustard, and olive oil and season with salt and pepper.
6. Fill the potato skins with the potato mixture. Top with parmesan and bake again until the cheese is melted and golden.
7. Top with a little yogurt, fresh chervil, and dill.

TIP: *You can use sour cream or cottage cheese instead of yogurt. Add other dried spices, garlic, chili, nutmeg, or dukkah for flavor.*

Medium

 6 people

 60 minutes

FILO PASTRY PIE
WITH SPINACH
(V) *and* **BROCCOLI**

200 g spinach
1 head broccoli
2 red onions
200 g cottage cheese
6 eggs
Grated nutmeg to taste
Salt and pepper to taste
1 packet filo pastry
3 tbsp. olive oil

1. Preheat the oven to 175°C/350°F.
2. Bring a pot of salted water to a boil.
3. Rinse the spinach and broccoli.
4. Peel and cut the red onions into 0.5-cm slices. Sauté until soft and translucent.
5. Cut the broccoli into small, bite-size pieces.
6. Blanch the broccoli in boiling water for approx. 10 seconds until it is cooked but still has bite and is beautifully green. Cool in cold water.
7. Place a layer of filo pastry on a thin ovenproof tray. Brush with olive oil and place the next layer on top, rotated 45°. Continue until you have four layers.
8. Beat the eggs together and season with salt, pepper, and finely grated nutmeg. Pour the egg mixture into the pan with the onions and warm over low-medium heat. The eggs should thicken a little but must not become scrambled. This way the pie bakes faster.
9. Mix the vegetables and cottage cheese with the egg mixture and fill the filo pastry with the filling. Make sure there are no air holes.
10. Curl up the filo pastry edges and brush with olive oil.
11. Bake for approx. 35–40 minutes or until the egg mass is firm and the filo pastry is a beautiful golden brown. During the first 20 minutes, a piece of foil must be placed over the pie so that it does not burn on top. The baking time depends on how tall your pie is.
12. Let the pie rest for approx. 10 minutes and serve it warm with a delicious little salad on the side.

TIP: *Use any vegetables you like for this pie, you can also add ham or leftover diced meat from dinner.*

PLAICE *with* TARTAR SAUCE

Ⓖ Ⓝ

300 g fillet of plaice (or any flatfish), **without skin**
100 g polenta or rye flour
1/2 bunch tarragon
1/2 bunch dill
50 g capers
50 g cornichons
1/2 red onion, chopped
100 g Greek yogurt
2 tbsp. mayonnaise
Juice and zest of 1 lemon
200 g broccolini
Olive oil for frying
Salt and pepper to taste

1. For the tartar sauce, blend the cornichons and capers into a thick sauce in a mini chopper. Add the onion and pulse until well mixed.
2. Finely chop the tarragon and dill and mix with the caper–cornichon sauce, yogurt, and mayonnaise in a bowl. Season with lemon zest and juice, salt, and pepper.
3. Fry the broccolini in a little olive oil and salt over high heat until it has color but is still beautifully green.
4. Season both sides of the fish with salt and pepper.
5. Coat the fillets with the polenta and fry them in a pan with olive oil over medium-high heat for 1 minute on each side or until golden brown.
6. Serve with the tartar sauce and broccolini.

TIP: *You can use breadcrumbs instead of polenta. Mix the breadcrumbs with herbs or a little paprika for extra flavor.*

STAGE

PIZZA *at*
PLACE DE LA CONCORDE

400 ml water
2 g dry yeast
500 g wheat flour
8 g salt
50 g sourdough (optional)
1 can chopped tomatoes
1 tbsp. balsamic vinegar
2 tbsp. olive oil
4 slices cooked ham
1 fresh mozzarella ball
50 g parmesan
1/2 bunch fresh basil
25 g pistacios

1. Dissolve the dry yeast and sourdough in the water.
2. Stir in the flour and salt and knead until the dough is firm.
3. Let the dough in a bowl for 30 minutes.
4. Fold the dough together and knead until pliable.
5. Divide the dough in half. Form 2 balls and let them rise, covered, in a warm place until they double in size.
6. Bring the canned tomatoes to a boil, season with salt and balsamic vinegar, and stir in the olive oil.
7. Preheat the oven to 240°C/460°F with a pizza stone or a baking tray turned upside down in the center of the oven.
8. With the dough, roll out 2 pizzas to approx. 25–30 cm/10-12 inches in diameter. Place them on separate pieces of baking paper.
9. Spread 2–3 spoonfuls of tomato sauce on each pizza base. Drizzle with a little olive oil and bake one at a time for approx. 8–10 minutes or until the base has set and is fully cooked and firm but without too much color. The pre-baked pizzas can be stored in the freezer or fridge for later use.
10. Top the first pre-baked pizza with parmesan and some small bits of mozzarella; leave a little mozzarella for the garnish. Bake the pizza again until the cheese has melted.
11. Top with ham, fresh mozzarella, basil and pistachio and serve with a glass of champagne.

TIP: *Make a pizza bianca by replacing the tomato sauce with mascarpone.*
Use any cold cuts of your preference or ad Italian sausage or nduja with the cheese when baking.

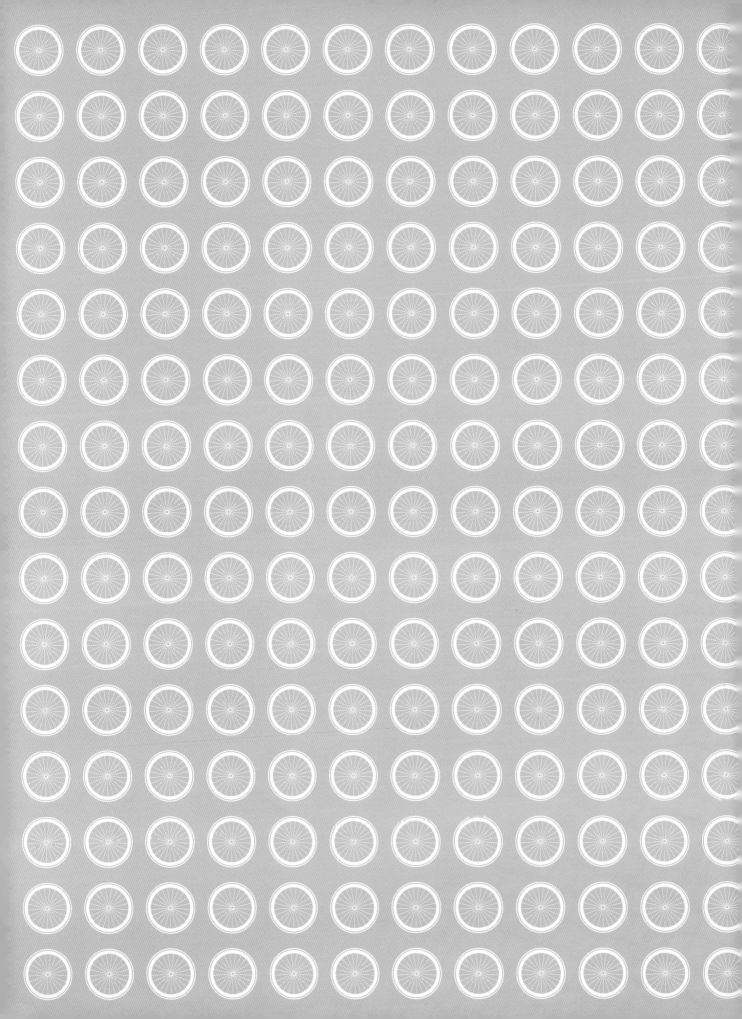

Race & snacks

RECOVERY MEALS

Race SNACKS

No two riders are the same, and what kind of snacks they prefer for a training ride varies. Here are a few suggestions for some easily prepared snacks to make for the long hours on the bike.

- Bananas
- Race cakes
- Watt the fudge cake – with or without fudge in the middle of 2 thin slices
- The yellow tour cake
- Lucky potato cake
- Lemon cake – with or without frosting in the middle of 2 thin slices
- Sandwiches with ham and cheese, peanut butter and banana, or chocolate fudge
- Raw bars
- Baked banana bars

CHOCOLATE FUDGE

12 pitted medjool dates
1 tbsp. unsweetened cocoa
100 ml boiling water
1/2 tsp. salt

1. Soak the dates in the boiling water.
2. Blend them with cocoa and salt.
3. Adjust any the texture with a little extra water and taste with salt and possibly a little cinnamon or finely grated orange zest.

RAW BAR – BASIC RECIPE

14–16 pitted medjool dates
140 g almonds or other nuts/seeds
2 tbsp. unsweetened cocoa powder
1/2 tsp. salt

1. Blend all the ingredients in a food processor.
2. Roll the mass into balls. Leave the raw bar balls in the fridge for an hour.

> **TIP:** *Flavor the bar with lime zest, orange zest, cinnamon, freeze-dried raspberries, etc., similar.*

BAKED BANANA BAR

2–3 bananas
200 g mixed muesli
2 tbsp. peanut butter
5 tbsp. maple syrup or honey
1/2 tsp. salt
Optional: Cinnamon, Chopped chocolate, Dried fruit, Protein powder

This recipe must be made according to the following motto: the softer the dough, the moister the bar and the longer the baking time. If you add protein powder, adjust the texture with more banana so that the bar does not become too dry.

1. Preheat the oven to 175°C/350°F.
2. Mash the bananas and mix with the rest of the ingredients in a bowl. Season to taste with salt and maple syrup.
3. Press the dough into a square baking tray lined with baking paper and bake until golden brown and firm. Cool completely before cutting.

> **TIP:** *Store the bars individually wrapped in the fridge or freezer so that you can grab a few on your way out the door.*

You can find a lot more delicious and race ready cake recipes in my other book, The Cake cookbook. You won't be disappointed.

RECOVERY *meals*

Here, we are talking about the recovery meal, which is eaten no later than 30–60 minutes after the end of training. After training, most riders drink a protein drink and eat leftovers from dinner, which typically consist of rice, quinoa, or pasta with vegetables and meat. Plenty of dishes from this book are perfect for this. Here are some examples:

- Fried rice with bulgogi sauce
- Fried noodles
- Quinoa bowl
- Pita bread or wraps with egg–tuna or chicken salad

- Roasted chicken and potatoes
- Chicken burritos

You can come up with many more variations yourself but just remember that you need to combine carbohydrates and protein.

RECOVERY PROTEIN DRINK

250 ml mælk, plantebaseret mælk
1 banan
1 spsk. peanutbutter
25 g proteinpulver – 1 scoop

Blend all ingredients, season with maple sirup and serve.

TIP: *You can add fruits and berries of y our choice. Keep in mind that your protein powder may have flavor or sweetener in it – I suggest getting a plain protein powder for the best results.*

Legendary
RICE BARS

Rice bars have become a stable food in the peloton. They are easy to make and can be varied in flavor as desired. You can make many variations, and they all start from the same basic recipe.

BASIC RICE BAR:
360 g sushi rice
720 ml water
1 tbsp. white or brown sugar
1 tsp. salt

1. Bring the rice to a boil with the sugar and salt, turn down the heat, and let simmer, covered, for approx. 20 minutes or until the water has been absorbed.
2. Fold in your desired flavorings and season with more salt and sugar to taste.
3. Press the rice into a mold lined with baking paper. Make sure the bars are approx. 2–3 cm thick. You can also press half of the rice into a mold, top with a layer of filling, and then add another layer of rice, like a sandwich.
4. Refrigerate the mold for at least 12 hours until the rice bars are firm. Cut into and pack them individually. You can keep them refrigerated for 4–5 days.

FLAVORINGS:

PEANUT BUTTER AND JELLY
Add approx. 30 g peanut butter and 30 g jam.

CHICKEN AND PARMESAN
Fold small cubes of cooked chicken breast and 30 g of grated parmesan to the rice mixture. Add 1 tbsp. cream cheese to make it creamier.

EGGS AND HAM
Scramble 2 eggs with small cubes of ham, season with salt, and stir into the rice mixture.

CHOCOLATE AND BANANA
Mix 30 g chopped chocolate and a sliced banana into the rice mixture. Add toasted, chopped nuts if you want a crunchy bite.

SWEET POTATO AND COTTAGE CHEESE
Add 50 g small cubes of baked sweet potato and 2 tbsp. cottage cheese to the rice mixture. Add fresh herbs if you like.

TIP: *Add fresh berries or small cubes of apple, pineapple, peach, and plums, raw or as a compote. Season with cinnamon or cinnamon fudge. You can also use my chocolate fudge. Get creative and let me know if you come up with something genious!*

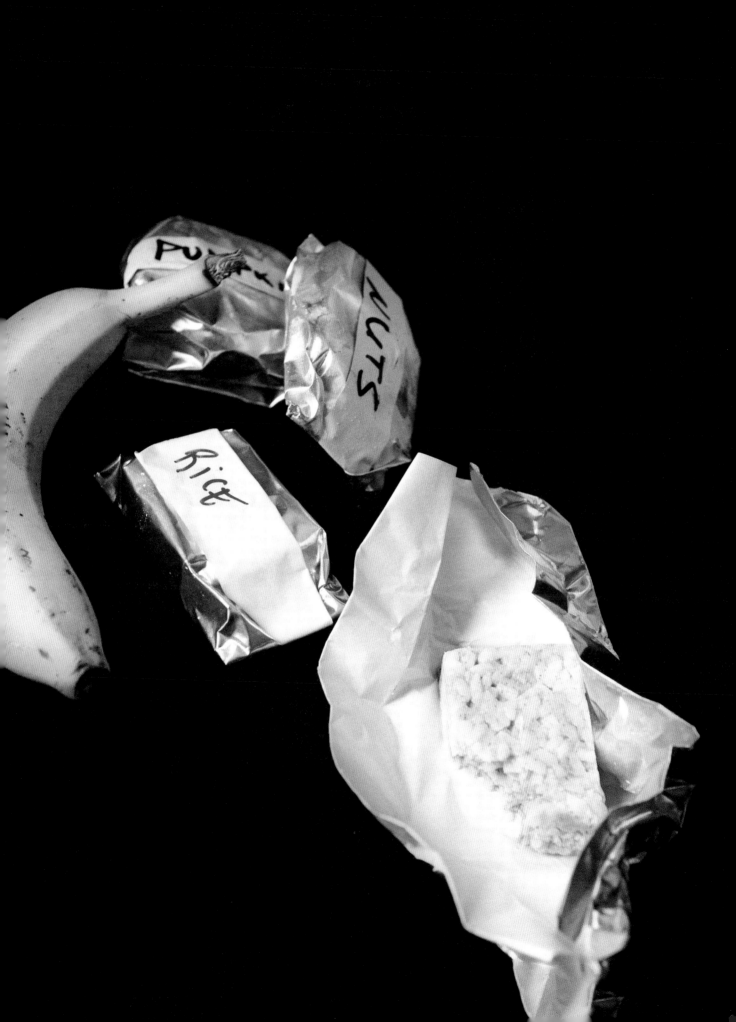

BREAK*fast*

GLOW UP *my* OATMEAL

Oatmeal can go in many delicious directions and be topped with anything the heart (and stomach) desires. All variations here start with the basic porridge or over-night version. You can use both rolled oats and fine oatmeal; just pay attention to the cooking time. If you like a firm porridge, you can use 50 ml less water. REMEMBER: Depending on what you top your porridge with, the allergens change accordingly.

 Easy

 5 minutes

 1 serving

 G D N V

BASIC PORRIDGE

35 g oatmeal
250 ml water
1 pinch salt

1. Bring all ingredients to a boil. Then, down the heat and let simmer, stirring frequently, for approx. 5 minutes.
2. Optional: add a mashed banana or a raw egg and heat through until the oatmeal starts to bubble.
3. If necessary, adjust the texture with a little extra water and season with salt and syrup.
4. Top with whatever you desire.

 Easy

 5 minutes + 12 hours in the fridge

 1 serving

G D V

BASIC REFRIGERATOR PORRIDGE - OVERNIGHT OATS

100 ml oatmeal
200 ml almond or regular milk
1 tbsp. maple syrup or honey
1 pinch salt
25 g nuts, seeds, or dried fruit (optional)
2 tbsp. Icelandic yogurt (skyr) or Greek yogurt

1. Mix the oatmeal, milk, syrup, salt, and seeds or nuts together and leave in the refrigerator overnight.
2. Before serving, stir in the yogurt and the desired filling, e.g., grated apple or blueberry.

Toppings:
Fresh fruit, berries, or grated carrot.
Fruit compote (diced fruit cooked with a little maple syrup or honey).
Nuts, kernels, or grits – preferably roasted.
Dried or freeze-dried fruit.
Peanut butter or any other nut butter.
Honey or maple syrup.

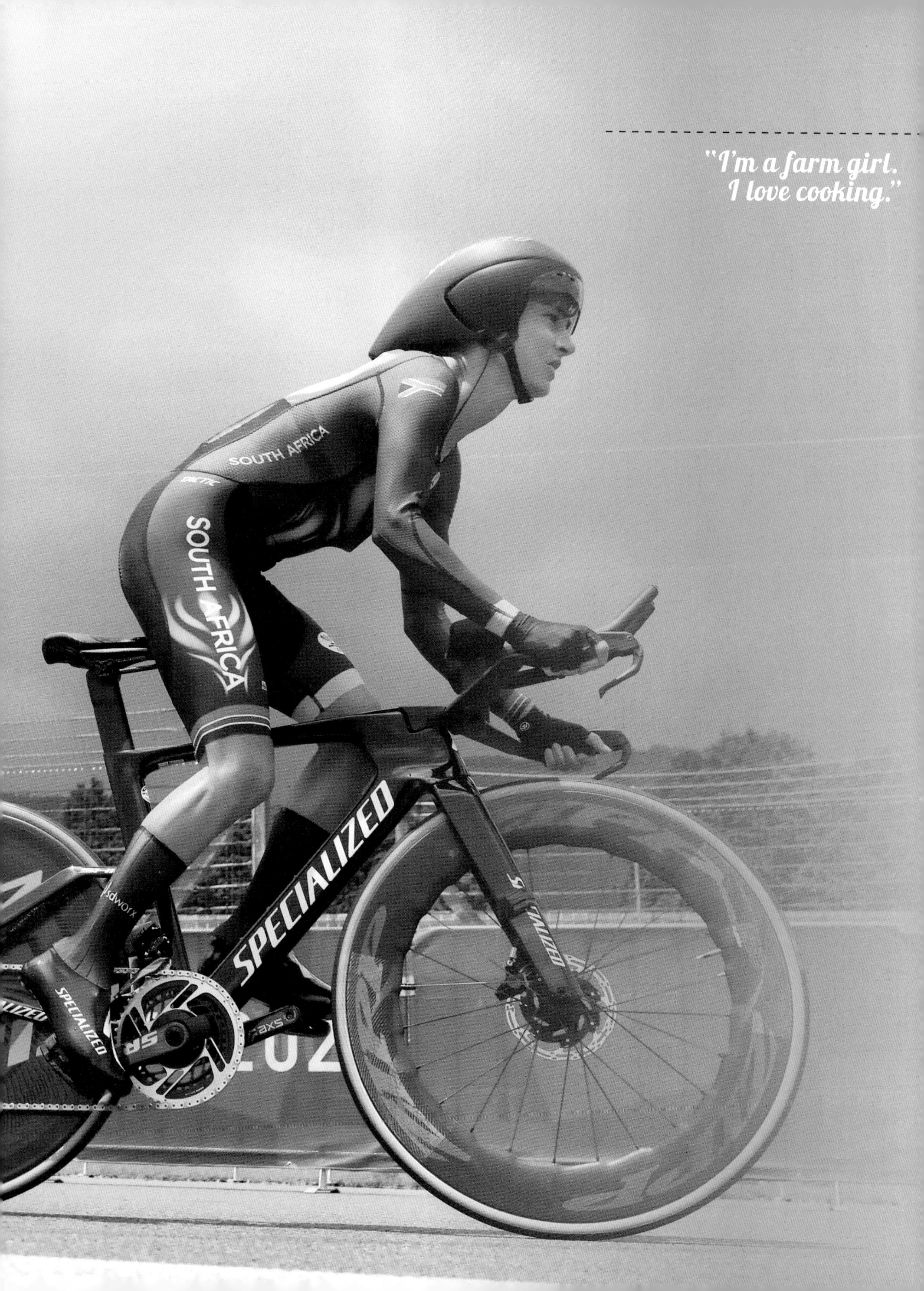

"I'm a farm girl. I love cooking."

ASHLEIGH MOOLMAN PASIO

Pro rider since 2010

Ashleigh Moolman is one of the best cyclists in the world. How she got there is a bit of a fairy-tale story, stemming from broken Olympic ambitions and stubbornness.

"I grew up in South Africa in a town called Bloemfontein. But we also had a family farm – my mom grew up on a farm just outside of Bloemfontein, in the Karoo, which is like a semi-desert area. I went to school in Bloemfontein, and it's a sort of small city in South Africa, but then I was pretty much a farm girl, you know, going to the farm just about every second weekend. And really I grew up riding horses, loving activity, loving exercise, really enjoying sport, but never really found the sport that I really excelled at in that school. Despite that, I had a dream of going to the Olympics one day."

However, no sport really caught her interest, and she did not excel in any of the popular school sports. As she grew up, she came to realize that going to the Olympics would likely be nothing but a distant dream.

"I left school and went to university thinking that's it, I'm not going to be a pro athlete, and I let go of the Olympic dream. And it was at university that I met my husband today, Carl. We studied at Stellenbosch University, just outside of Cape Town. And he introduced me to the endurance sporting disciplines. He was a triathlete at the time that I met him, but he came from a background of bike racing and triathlons growing up. And so, it was this new guy that I was really into, and I thought, well, how am I going to

impress him? So I set the challenge of, you know, okay, you're a triathlete, and you ride, I want to do it too. On our first holiday at university, he invited me to go home with him to his hometown, which is Niceness, it's about five hours up the coast from Cape Town. I didn't actually have a racing bike or anything at the time, so I borrowed my mom's bike. I took it to his home, and I rocked up with just my sneakers and my shorts and a T-shirt, but I was still up for the challenge. So I joined him on a ride, and we finished the ride after going up quite a steep climb in his hometown. And his dad was also with us, at that time. And when we got home, I overheard them talking and his dad saying to him, you know, that girl, she's got a talent for riding. Did you see her go up that climb?"

As it turned out, her path to being a pro rider would not be a traditional one. On her 21st birthday, she had only an entry-level aluminum bike. But that soon changed.

"It was sort of a family tradition – at the age of 21, my dad would buy us a car. He bought my sister, my oldest sister, a car for her 21st birthday. So of course I had that option as well, you know. He said 'when you're 21, I'll buy you a second-hand car, so you'll have wheels'. But at that time, I was already moving my way up in the cycling world, so I wanted a carbon race bike instead – my entry-level aluminum bike wasn't good enough any longer. So I got the bike from my dad, and that's when things really started taking off, and I started to become really competitive locally, riding my bike. I developed my talent throughout my university career. And then, in my final year, that's when I really realized, okay, now I'm winning bike races in South Africa, and I really started to see this potential that it could be a career. Because in the early days, when Carl used to say to me, you could be one of the best cyclists in the world, I thought he was crazy."

In the summer of 2012, her dream came true: she competed in the 2012 Summer Olympics Road Race. She soon realized that being a strong rider was about more than just climbs and embarked on a personal nutrition journey.

"I've always loved food and cooking food. As I said, I grew up on a farm, I was a real farm girl, and it was all about cooking nice big meals to share together. I think I under-ate and under-drank on the bike for many years, and it's something that I've only managed to really get a grip on later in my career. Because I suppose there was also sort of a trend in those cycling years, where less is more because there was all this focus on weight, and people thought that you had to really cut your calories to achieve those weight targets. Whereas now, there's a lot more information around saying that, actually, more is better and that we're burning so many calories on the bike that we can afford to be eating a lot of food."

This change in her understanding of nutrition was not only about accepting the amounts of food required, but also a cultural and identity change, she says.

"The mentality is shifting now. In a way, women's cycling, I would say, is almost healthier than men's cycling, and the reason why I say that is because I think women's cycling is creating an identity that is much healthier. You know, because of the nature of our racing, and the fact that we don't necessarily have such long races, or go up such crazy long climbs or get a crazy amount of altitude in a race, it means that our racing is better suited to the all-rounder. The role models in women's cycling are generally strong, healthy-looking women, because strength comes into the equation more than just the power-to-weight ratio."

"I think women's cycling is genuinely in a healthier space than men's cycling, and the body image of the role models is definitely healthier."

Pro riders have an attitude of 'lose weight, be happy'. However, Ashleigh Moolman discovered that there are sometimes reasons to put on weight."

"As I've gotten older, I've also realized, as a cyclist, that it's good to put on some weight in the off-season. Because, number one, it's good for your mental well-being to eat what you like or have some wine if you want. I'm comfortable with putting on some weight in the offseason. Then, the weight that I aim to achieve for the classics is a different weight than what I would aim for on the Grand Tours. At the classics, I don't need to be as light, because it's short steep climbs – weight is not as big a factor, it's more about power and being strong. And also, there could be benefits to being slightly heavier. Because you never know what the weather's going to be like. You know, if it's going to be super cold, you don't want to be super skinny. So that's how I treat it. And then the Grand Tours is when I want to be the most aggressive with my weight."

What does a day of eating look like when Ashleigh Moolman is home and doing interval training?

"I love breakfast, it's my favorite meal. So I'd never skip breakfast, and I love something sweet for breakfast. It's very difficult for me to start with savory stuff, it just doesn't sit well with me. I mean, I love eggs, for example, or brunch-style stuff, but I don't crave them first thing in the morning. So usually my breakfast would be muesli with yogurt and fresh fruit, or it's oatmeal, like an apple pie version of oatmeal with apples and raisins in, and maybe some nut butter. I have another really nice alternative where it's oatmeal with mashed-up banana and cocoa, so it's more like a chocolatey version. I usually have that plus coffee, which is non-negotiable, especially in the morning. My day does not start without a coffee. I'd usually wait an hour and a half, maybe two hours before I head out on the ride."

When she gets back from an interval ride, she feels tired and like she doesn't have a lot of energy left to spend a long time preparing a meal.

"I try to be a bit proactive. Whenever I'm cooking dinner at night, I try to cook a little bit extra, or if I'm roasting vegetables to eat at nighttime, I roast a lot more, so that I have them the next day as well. And then I'm a big one for like, these bowls. So, maybe it's like roast veggies with goat's cheese, and quinoa and kale – that's something that comes quickly to mind because it's one of my favorites. That is the type of thing I usually eat for lunch."

Dinner is time for fueling up on proteins, she says.

"It would usually be some form of meat; I try and mix it up through the week. So fish or chicken or beef or lamb – I quite like lamb, which not everybody likes. I try and mix it up over the course of the week. If I'm really starting to get close to race season, where I want to be sure that I'm hitting my race weight, then I'm a bit more particular around making sure that it's – well, not bland, but that I'm not having a lot of sauces and stuff like that."

Weighing food is popular in road racing, but Ashleigh Moolman is not a fan of this strategy for many reasons.

"I don't weigh my food, I go by experience. I know what I need. Of course, at times, maybe when I'm really needing to hit a certain weight target, I have to be a little bit more conscious, but I try not to get too caught up in it. So, I think, again, it comes with time and maturity and age, you start to get a real feel for it. I don't like to have to bring up the scale and weigh. But with experience you start to get an idea, you know what I mean, in your mind. You start to realize what a certain amount of food represents in terms of calories and what you can and can't eat. And for me, the big secret in terms of – I like to stay kind of healthy, well-

balanced throughout the year. But I think the real trick is, when you're trying to be more aggressive, I actually think a lot of people underestimate those hidden calories when it comes to sauces or sugars or even nut butter."

"So, maybe closer to the race, or when I'm trying to be more aggressive, then I have to think a little bit about 'okay, maybe I shouldn't have that tablespoon or loaded tablespoon of almond butter in my breakfast', to let that one slide. But I don't weigh food or measure out food. I try to do it by feel and by eye."

There are also other reasons, she says. At the races she attends, female riders do not have their food weighed out, despite this being a massive trend in the men's races.

"[Weighing food] isn't happening in women's cycling just yet. And I don't really foresee it coming into women's cycling, because of that concern that it's going to lead to disorders. I have to be honest, there are times, especially when it comes to Grand Tours, when I do feel like, should I be doing that? Just because a Grand Tour is quite a tricky thing. We only do stage races over eight to 10 days. The men do a Grand Tour for three weeks. And in week three, you start to not even have an appetite. I don't even want to know how they get through it. That, I think, is a more sensitive space. Because I think that when you start losing your appetite for food, then there's a possibility that you might not eat enough, especially in women's racing, because our calorie demands and our energy demands aren't quite as big as the men's."

"Then again, this is my 14th season in the pro peloton, and I still haven't, like I said, completely mastered the nutrition side of the sport. There are times when I wonder, am I eating enough? Am I eating too much? So, I think there could be a place for being a little bit more specific and controlled when it comes to stage racing."

Easy

4 people

60 minutes

Baked PORRIDGE
WITH PINEAPPLE

(G) (D) (N) (V)

150 g pineapple
4 pitted medjool dates
175 g oatmeal
1 tsp. baking soda
1/2 tsp. salt
2 tsp. breakfast spice
500 ml plant or regular milk
2 eggs
50 ml maple syrup or honey

Breakfast spice:
2 tbsp. ground ginger
2 tbsp. grated nutmeg
2 tbsp. ground cinnamon
2 tbsp. cardamom

1. Preheat the oven to 180°C/360°F.
2. Cut the pineapple into small cubes and chop the dates.
3. Mix all ingredients together and pour into a cast iron pan or an ovenproof dish.
4. Bake, covered, for 30 minutes. Then, remove the covering and finish baking. It should be golden brown and delicious.
5. Serve with maple syrup and top with skyr or yogurt if desired.

Breakfast spice:
Mix all spices store in an airtight container.

TIP: *Add grated coconut to the mixture.*
You can make this porridge with all kinds of fruits, berries, nuts, and seeds. You can also make a carrot cake version by adding grated carrot and raisins instead of pineapple and dates. This dish also tastes great cold and can be eaten as a recovery meal.

Easy

 12 pancakes

 25 minutes

GLUTEN-FREE PANCAKES

Ⓖ Ⓝ Ⓥ *and* FRUIT SALAD

3 eggs
250 ml plant or regular milk
3 tbsp. maple syrup
1/2 tsp. xanthan gum or psyllium husks
50 g rice flour
50 g oat flour (finely blended oatmeal)
1 tsp. fine salt
50 g regular or vegan butter + a little extra for frying
1 orange
1/2 tray strawberries
1 apple
1 banana
3-4 mint leaves
100 g skyr or yogurt

1. Whisk the eggs, milk, and maple syrup together.
2. Stir the xanthan gum or psyllium husks into the liquid and let sit for 2–3 minutes while you weigh out the dry ingredients.
3. Mix the rice flour and oat flour in a bowl with the salt.
4. Melt the butter over low heat.
5. Sift the flour mixture into the egg mixture and beat into a smooth batter.
6. Whisk in the melted butter and let rest for 5 minutes before frying.
7. Cut the fruit into small cubes. Chop the mint and mix it with the fruit.
8. Heat a small pan over medium-high heat. Grease with a small lump of butter.
9. Pour approx. 50 ml batter on the pan. Use a small spatula to carefully spread out the batter.
10. Fry the pancake on both sides over medium heat until golden brown and delicious.
11. Keep warm under foil while you finish the rest of the pancakes.
12. Serve topped with fruit salad, skyr or yogurt, and maple syrup.

TIP: *Fold the pancakes into quarters with jam or cinnamon fudge and take them with you on a training trip.*

INFO: *Xanthan gum is an emulsifier that is used in gluten-free bread and pastries to replace the chemical effect of gluten. Xanthan gum and psyllium husks make the batter easier to work with so that the pancake becomes soft. You don't have to use it in the recipe, but the pancakes will crack easily after being cooked.*

Easy 1 person

 5 minutes

THE TOUR SMOOTHIE

200 g fruit or vegetables
100 ml plant or regular milk
50 ml skyr, yogurt, or vegan yogurt
2 tbsp. maple syrup or honey
Lemon juice to taste

No breakfast table is complete without a smoothie, which can pimp up any breakfast. Every morning during the tour, rice or pasta with eggs is on the menu, but since you don't need a recipe for boiled rice with scrambled eggs, you get a tour smoothie recipe so that you can make delicious smoothies for the breakfast table. This is a basic recipe with many variations so that you can make your favorites. Blend all ingredients and season with syrup and lemon juice. If necessary, adjust the texture with a little extra liquid.

Variationer
– Mango and strawberry with mint
– Pineapple, ginger, cinnamon, and banana
– Raspberry and banana with orange
– Cocoa, banana, and peanut butter
– Avocado, mango, and lime
– Kiwi, spinach, and banana

You can create many more variations yourself.

TIP: *You can also make a smoothie bowl using frozen bananas and lower the amount of liquid used slightly. Top with everything from the Pimp my porridge recipe.*
You can also blend in dried spices, such as allspice or cardamom. Add protein powder. Don't forget to consider whether your protein powder is sweetened and that the amount of liquid must be increased slightly.

Brown bananas: *You must never throw out a brown banana – they're edible gold in a smoothie. Skin and freeze brown bananas in a box so that you can easily take one out when you need to make a smoothie.*

All that **EQUALLY** IMPORTANT STUFF

6.30

7.00

8.00

9.00

10.00

BOIL an EGG

Everyone who eats eggs has an opinion on how much or how little the egg should be cooked. I personally like a completely soft egg, but that's why you should be allowed to cook it as you desire.

There are many ways to boil eggs, but I think this method has the most consistent results every time. You can see in the picture exactly how long the egg has cooked.

The eggs I've used weigh around 55 g each, so the cooking times have been adjusted accordingly. As a general rule, for every 5 g more or less than 55 g that your egg weighs, you must adjust the time by approx. 15 seconds up or down, respectively.

Weigh a few eggs from your egg tray and then cook 1 egg according to the instructions. Cool, peel, and cut it to judge whether the eggs need more or less cooking time. Feel free to note it down here in the book. Then, you'll know exactly how to cook your eggs.

HOW TO DO IT

1. Bring a pot of water to a boil. There must be enough water for the egg(s) to be properly covered.
2. IMPORTANT: Set a timer to the desired number of minutes and seconds and then lower the eggs into the boiling water. Start the timer immediately. Turn the heat down so that the egg doesn't jump around wildly but the water is still boiling.
3. When the timer sounds, take out the eggs and drop them into a bowl of cold water to stop the cooking. If your eggs don't cool down fast enough, they will become firmer and overcooked.
4. Peel and serve.

   TIP: *You can also serve the eggs warm straightaway, but I still recommend that you drop them in cold water to stop the worst of the post cooking.*

You can easily cook many eggs at a time; however, the cooking time will be extended a little since placing many eggs in it the water will lower the temperature and make it take longer to boil. You can use a larger pot with plenty of water so that the water keeps boiling. Keep the boiled eggs in the fridge for up to a week so that they are ready for you when you're hungry.

LET IT *sprout*

Why should you sprout your own seeds, grains and peas? In addition to the fantastic joy of watching something grow, you also get a delicious, crisp nutrient bomb on your plate, which can spice up any dish.

How to sprout seeds, grains and peas: When a seed is soaked in water under the right conditions, it begins to germinate. There are some simple rules you must follow to get the best results. Always use a transparent container and make sure that air can enter it during the germination process. The container must be kept out of direct sunlight and at room temperature. Chickpeas grow in size, so your container should be at least 3–4 times larger than the volume of the soaked chickpeas. Use a measuring cup for the chickpeas and water.

SPROUTED CHICKPEAS
1 part chickpeas
3 parts water

1. **Soaking:** Rinse the chickpeas in water and let them soak in cold water for 12 hours or overnight.
2. **Cleaning:** Remove any small parts floating in the water. Sieve the chickpeas and rinse them well under running cold water. Drain them well and put them back in the container. Cover with a cloth or lid on but make sure that air can still get in. Rinse the chickpeas carefully in the morning and evening every day until they have sprouted. It takes 3–5 days for chickpeas to germinate. The longer you repeat this process, the bigger the sprouts. Taste them daily.
3. **Drain and pack:** Once the chickpeas sprouts have grown to the desired size, rinse and drain the chickpeas well so that there is no water at the bottom of the container. Pack them in an airtight container and refrigerate for 4–6 weeks.
4. Serve raw or slightly warmed.

TIP: *Always use organic seeds and peas to be sure you have the purest, highest-quality product.*

You can germinate all sorts of seeds and peas using the same process as above; however, the soaking and germination times will be different. Here is a non-exhaustive list:

Pumpkin seeds: Soak 1–4 hours. Rinse twice daily. They will be ready within 1–2 days.

Sunflower seeds: Soak 1–2 hours. Rinse twice daily. They will be ready within 1–2 days.

Buckwheat kernels: Soak 30 minutes. Rinse twice daily very thoroughly to get the starch out. They will be ready within 1–3 days.

Yellow peas: Soak 8–12 hours. Rinse 2–3 times daily. They will be ready within 2–3 days.

Mung beans: Soak 8–12 hours. Rinse twice daily. They will be ready within 2–5 days

Green lentils: Soak 8–12 hours. Rinse twice daily. They will be ready within 2–3 days.

SPROUTED CHICKPEAS *with*
AVOCADO, APPLE, & TAINI DRESSING

G M N V

100 g sprouted chickpeas
1 avocado
1 apple
2 tsp. liquid light tahini
1 tsp. liquid honey
1/2 garlic clove
Juice of 1/2 lemon
1 tbsp. mild olive oil
Salt to taste

1. Rinse your sprouts.
2. Cut the avocado and apple into wedges.
3. Stir the tahini with the pressed garlic, lemon juice, salt, and olive oil. Add salt and lemon juice to taste and adjust the texture with a little water if necessary.
4. Serve the sprouts and top with the tahini dressing.

Easy 2 pieces

 14 hours

GLUTEN FREE *bread*

175 g oat flour (finely blended oatmeal)
225 g rice flour
500 g plant or regular milk
2 tbsp. olive oil
1 tbsp. maple syrup or honey
10 g fine salt
10 g yeast
15 g psyllium husk
2 eggs
100 g mixed seeds

This is a recipe with several variations. Follow the basic recipe and make a nice basic bread, delicious focaccia, or soft burger buns.

1. Combine the flours together.
2. Stir all the liquid ingredients together and dissolve the yeast in the mixture.
3. Whisk the mixture with the psyllium husks and leave too steep for approx. 5 minutes.
4. Stir the flour and liquid mixtures together and leave the dough covered for in the fridge for at least 3–4 hours or overnight, until the dough has set.
5. Preheat the oven to 225°C/440°F.
6. Line a baking tray with baking paper. Use a large spoon to scoop out bread roll sized scoops of dough. Flip them in the mixed seeds and place them on the baking tray.
7. Bake for approx. 20-25 minutes or until the bread is golden brown and sounds hollow when tapped.

Bake a basic bread
Mix the dough as instructed above. Add 50 g of any nuts or seeds before the dough rises. Place the dough into a loaf tin lined with baking paper and sprinkle with seeds. Bake for approx. 35 minutes or until the bread is golden brown and sounds hollow when tapped.

Burger buns
1. Mix the dough as instructed above. At step 5, line 8 coffee cups with plastic film, grease them with a little oil, and fill the cups with the dough.
2. Let rest in the fridge overnight.
3. Turn the buns out onto a baking sheet lined with baking paper and sprinkled with a little flour.
4. Bake the buns for 10–12 minutes or until firm.
5. Whisk an egg and brush the buns with it. Sprinkle with white sesame seeds.
6. Turn the heat down to 200°C/390°F and bake for another 10 minutes or until the buns are golden brown and sound hollow when tapped.

HOMEMADE *pasta*

There's no getting around the fact that pasta is one of the dishes riders eat the most, and that's why I've chosen to give you the opportunity to make your very own fresh pasta. Of course, you can always replace homemade fresh pasta with a delicious supermarket version, be it dry or fresh.

Many riders have a very strong opinion about pasta, right down to the detail of which shape they prefer and how long it should be cooked. According to my statistics, most riders are happiest with al dente pasta, or pasta with a little bit of bite. Of course, you decide for yourself how you want to cook it.

Here, you get three basic recipes for a classic pasta dough with eggs, one without eggs, and a gluten-free version with eggs so that you can enjoy the pasta dishes in the book even if you don't eat wheat flour.

Before we get started, make sure you have a pasta machine or some good Italian grandma rolling skills. That way, the pasta will definitely be the best. You can start by borrowing your neighbor's pasta machine.

TYPES OF FLOUR
Flour is categorized according to how high its gluten content is and, overall, can be divided into hard and soft flour.

Durum flour and semolina durum are hard. Hard flour has a high gluten content and is best suited for pasta dough without eggs, as the gluten content in the flour makes the dough elastic and flexible. This type of dough is typically slightly tougher to work with and can be a little more demanding to handle.

Tipo 0 and Tipo 00 are the soft types of flour, with a lower gluten content and a finer grinding degree. These types of flour are best suited for pasta dough with eggs. The gluten content is low, and the dough therefore needs help from the egg to soften the dough.

WHAT IS GLUTEN?
Gluten is a collection of proteins. It is found in many grains, including wheat, rye, barley, and spelt. When flour is mixed with water, the gluten proteins are activated and form a structure that gives the dough its elasticity and strength. The more the dough is kneaded, the more the gluten proteins develop a networked structure. As a result, the dough becomes much more flexible, which is good when making pasta. Gluten protein also plays a big role in bread baking, and the higher the gluten content of bread dough, the larger the air holes it can contain, making it crisp and giving the bread bite.

Gluten-free flours are a completely different category, as they do not contain gluten. Here, a little extra help is needed to make the dough stick together. In the gluten-free pasta recipe below, I use flour types without a strong taste to get a pasta dough that tastes as close to regular pasta as possible. Eggs and xanthan gum are added to the dough to ensure that the dough does not break down before or after cooking. Xanthan gum is made by fermenting carbohydrates with a special type of bacteria. You may have seen this process if you have ever grabbed a vegetable with slime on it. When a vegetable has a nick or dent in it, a slime layer forms on top of the damaged part to protect it. That slime layer is made by the bacteria used to make xanthan gum. You can buy xanthan gum in well-stocked supermarkets or online shops.

PASTA DOUGH WITH EGGS

600 g Tipo 00
300 g whole eggs
1 pinch salt

PASTA DOUGH WITHOUT EGGS

600 g semolina durum
300 ml water
1 pinch fine salt

GLUTEN-FREE PASTA DOUGH

300 g fine rice flour
100 g potato flour
2 tbsp. cornstarch
4 tbsp. xanthan gum
6 whole eggs
2 tbsp. olive oil
1/2 tsp. fine salt

You can make the pasta dough by hand or with a machine.

BY HAND (use this method for dough with or without eggs; the water replaces the eggs):

1. Sift the flour into a bowl and then pour it out onto a clean surface or into a very large bowl. Make a hole in the middle.
2. Beat the eggs in a bowl. Season with salt, whisk, and pour into the hole in the flour.
3. Using a fork or your hand, mix the flour and egg together by gradually incorporating more and more flour into the egg mixture from the sides.
4. Gather the dough with your hands and knead it for approx. 10–15 minutes or until smooth and elastic.
5. Pasta dough with eggs must rest for 30 minutes. Pasta dough without eggs can be used immediately.

WITH A FOOD PROCESSOR (works for all types of dough):

1. Blend all ingredients into a lumpy dough in the food processor.
2. Knead the dough by hand for approx. 5 minutes.
3. Pasta dough with eggs must rest for 30 minutes. Gluten-free pasta dough and dough without eggs can be used immediately.

WITH A MIXER (works for all types of dough):

1. Mix all ingredients in the mixer.
2. Knead the dough for approx. 5 minutes at low speed.
3. Pasta dough with eggs must rest for 30 minutes. Gluten-free pasta dough and dough without eggs can be used immediately.

ROLLING OUT THE DOUGH

Divide the dough into four equal parts. To start, roll out the dough by hand so that it is flat enough to pass through the pasta machine on the thickest setting. Then, roll it through the pasta machine.

Start on the highest setting. Once you've rolled the dough through once, fold it in half and roll it through again. Repeat this process until the dough is elastic and firm. The dough will be gradually rolled thinner each time it passes through the machine. The thinner it's rolled, the shorter the cooking time.

> **NOTE:** *Gluten-free dough can be a bit crumbly. Be patient because it should come together after you've run it through the pasta machine a few times. It should not be rolled too thin. Roll it using setting 4 of the pasta machine.*

SAUCES *and* DRESSINGS

The procedure is the same for all dressings; only the measurements and ingredients change. Keep the dressings in air tight containers in the fridge for up to three weeks.

1. Whisk together all wet ingredients and flavorings, except for the oil.
2. Whisk in the oil a little at a time.
3. Season to taste with salt and more of the acidic and sweet ingredients if necessary.

DRESSINGS:

DIJON DRESSING

1 tsp. Dijon mustard
2 tsp. white wine or red wine vinegar
1 tbsp. maple syrup/honey
1/2 tsp. salt
6 tbsp. olive oil

BALSAMIC HONEY DRESSING

2 tbsp. balsamic vinegar
1 tbsp. honey
1/2 tsp. salt
1/2 garlic clove, grated or pressed (optional)
3 tbsp. olive oil

MUSTARD AND HONEY DRESSING

2 tbsp. coarse grain mustard
2 tbsp. honey
Juice of 1 small lemon
1/2 tsp. salt
6 tbsp. olive oil

TAHINI DRESSING

3 tbsp. liquid light tahini
Juice of 1/2 lemon
3 tbsp. water
1 tbsp. maple syrup or honey
1 small garlic clove
Salt and pepper to taste
1 tbsp. olive oil

SOY SESAME DRESSING

2 tbsp. soy sauce
2 tsp. toasted sesame oil
Juice and zest of 1 lime
1 tbsp. maple syrup
2 tbsp. oil
Chili to taste

SAUCES:

HOULE FUEL

3 tbsp. sriracha sauce
3 tbsp. maple syrup
3 tbsp. soy sauce
2 tbsp. rice wine or white wine vinegar

1. Boil all ingredients. Let cool and refrigerate.
2. Serve with fish, chicken, rice, or vegetables.

VIETNAMESE COLD SAUCE

2 tbsp. sesame oil
Juice of 1 lime
1 tsp. fish sauce
1 tbsp. honey
Fresh or dried chili, fresh coriander, or mint (optional)

Mix all ingredients together and serve with salads, meat, fish, or rice.

AVOCADO LIME SAUCE

1 avocado
1 small garlic clove
100 ml skyr or yogurt
Juice and zest of 2 limes
Salt to taste

*Blend all ingredients until smooth. Adjust the
texture with a little water if necessary.*

PAN ROASTED TOMATO SAUCE

500 g small tomatoes
1 garlic clove, grated or pressed
1 tbsp. balsamic vinegar
1 tsp. honey
Salt and pepper to taste
2 tbsp. olive oil

1. Rinse the tomatoes, dry them well, and place
   them in a hot, heavy-bottomed pan with the
   olive oil and salt.
2. Cook the tomatoes, covered, for approx. 10
   minutes or until they are punctured and have
   a little color on the bottom.
3. Add the honey, balsamic vinegar, and
   garlic and heat through.
4. Blend with a stick blender and season
   with salt and vinegar. You can also
   mash the sauce together with a fork.
5. Serve with meat, fish, vegetables, or pasta.

   TIP: *Add fresh basil, oregano, thyme, or
   rosemary.*

STOCK
and PICKLE LIQUIDS

I love a good stock, and I think it's worth the time to make. I have a pressure cooker, which makes stock super easy and quick to make. Alternatively, you can make it in a pot in the oven – it will take care of itself.

You can make the basic recipe with chicken/duck scraps or veal/beef/lamb legs. I store the chicken scraps in the freezer every time we eat chicken so that I can make stock whenever I have enough scraps. Many supermarkets also have frozen beef and veal legs or you can support your local butcher.

BASE STOCK IN OVEN
1.5 kg scraps or legs
2 large carrots
2 celery stalks
2 onions
4 garlic cloves
1 tsp. coriander seeds
1 tsp. black pepper
1 star anise (optional)
4 bay leaves
2500 ml water
1 tbsp. olive oil

1. Preheat the oven to 175°C.
2. Place the meat/scraps in a large cast iron pan, pressing them together so they fit.
3. Peel all vegetables and chop them into rough pieces. Mix with 1 tbsp. oil and place with the scraps.
4. Roast in the oven, uncovered, for 1 hour until nicely cooked.
5. Add the spices and water, cover, and cook for 2 hours. Keep an eye on it – you may need to top up with a little water along the way, as the scraps should be covered at all times.
6. Sift the stock, bring it to a boil, and skim off the fat.
7. Pour the stock into 250-ml containers or bags and refrigerate or freeze.

> **TIP:** *You can use all kinds of root vegetables, except beetroot, for the base stock.*
> *Add fresh thyme, rosemary, or similar herbs during the last hour of the cooking time. You can also make the stock on the stove. Keep an eye on it and top up with water as needed. You can skim off fat along the way.*
> *To make a light stock, don't roast the ingredients; rather, add the water immediately.*

BASE STOCK IN A PRESSURE COOKER
1. Brown all ingredients in a hot pan for a few minutes and then transfer to a pressure cooker.
2. Pour in water to the safety line, put the lid on, and pressurize. Turn the heat down and leave to pressure cook for 30 minutes for chicken and 1 hour for beef legs. Once finished, let the valve open by itself. Then, continue from step 6 above.

VEGETABLE STOCK

500 g mushrooms
2 large carrots
2 celery stalks
2 onions
1 whole garlic clove, cut crosswise
1 tsp. coriander seeds
1 tsp. black pepper
1 star anise (optional)
4 bay leaves
2 tbsp. tomato paste
1500 ml water

1. Clean all vegetables and chop them into rough pieces.
2. Brown them in a frying pan with a little oil until they get a nice, caramelized color.
3. Pour in the water and bring to a boil. Turn down the heat and let simmer for 1 hour.
4. Sift the stock and boil it down to half its original volume.
5. Let cool. Then, portion it out and refrigerate or freeze.

> **TIP:** *Add dried Karl Johan mushrooms or shiitake mushrooms to get an extra-delicious umami bomb of a stock.*

Make small super tasty stock packages. When the stock is done, you can boil it down to half or even 1/3 of its original volume and freeze it in ice cube trays that you can store in the freezer like super tasty flavor bombs. Then, you'll always have a delicious stock cube on hand for soups and sauces that just need a little extra flavor.

PICKLE LIQUID

Make your own pickled vegetables with the 1:1:1 guideline:

100 ml vinegar
100 ml water
100 g sugar

1. Mix all ingredients, bring to a boil in a pot, and let cool.
2. Pour over the sliced greens and let the pickles soak in the refrigerator for at least 12 hours. Alternatively, pour the hot stock over the vegetables immediately and let them soak for 30 minutes before serving; this will make the vegetables a little softer.

> **TIP:** *Add spices and herbs. You can pickle onions, cabbage, cucumbers, and other crispy greens.*

BEEF BROTH

RECIPE INDEX

Ⓖ GLUTEN FREE A-Z

ALL RECIPES A-Z SORTED BY TYPE

SALADS, VEGGIES AND STARTERS A-Z

MAIN COURSES A-Z

Seared tuna with nectarines and leche de tigre | 94
Sheetpan ratatouille with chickpeas | 284
Stir-fry noodles with beef and veggies | 50
Veal piccata | 150

MEAT AND FISH A-Z

BBQ chicken | 196
Butter chicken | 186
Chicken and mozzarella in tomato sauce | 72
Chicken burritos | 210
Chicken salad with apple, tarragin and pickled red onion | 236
Coq au vin blanc | 266
Corts SMASH burger | 220
Delicious all-round meat balls | 252
Fish burger | 222
Flank steak with baked tomatoes and chimichurri | 134
Gyodon - Rice with minced beef and fried egg | 122
Houle Fuel Chicken and mango salad | 48
Juicy roasted chicken with potato and onion | 242
Kofta with courgette and quinoa | 278
Leg of lamb, parsleysalad and yoghurt sauce | 88
Mads P's lasagna | 288
Not a time trial pasta ragù | 174
Pan fired cod with tangy salsa | 64
Peanut chicken | 98
Pink ginger rice with sashimi salmon | 118
Pizza | 308
Plaice with tartar sauce | 304
Pork cheeks and polenta | 164
pork chops plums and green herb sauce | 44
Quesedilla | 214
Salmon fish cakes with red coleslaw | 172
Salmon foil packs with herbs and white wine | 114
Seared tuna with nectarines and leche de tigre | 94
Smoked salmon with mozzarella and blueberries | 238
Stir-fry noodles with beef and veggies | 50
Tuna- and egg salad with pear | 286
Veal piccata | 150

CARBS AND STARCHES A-Z

Baked porridge with pineapple | 324
Baked sweet potato with goat cheese creme and dukkah | 62
Béarnaise potato salad | 194
Carbonara with chervil and asparagus | 144
Cecilie's Dhal | 250

Chickpea curry with fried spring onion | 182
Crispy smashed potaoes | 262
Double-baked jacket poatoes | 300
Dutch oven bread | 142
Falafel-waffle | 276
Fried rice with bulgogi sauce | 112
Gluten free bread | 336
Gluten free pasta dough | 338
Gluten-free pancakes with fruit salad | 326
Green summer salad with potatoes | 132
Gyodon - Rice with minced beef and fried egg | 122
Houle Fuel Chicken and mango salad | 48
Mads P's lasagna | 288
Mads P's pancakes | 290
Mashed potatoes with herbs | 148
Pasta dough with eggs | 338
Pasta dough without eggs | 338
Pasta Marinara withfresh tomatoes | 42
Pasta Romesco | 268
Pasta with lemon- and mint pesto | 162
Pimp my oatmeal | 318
Pink ginger rice with sashimi salmon | 118
Pita bread | 90
Pizza at Place de la Concorde | 308
Plant based bolognaise | 96
Quinoa-bowl | 70
Rice, rice baby | 274
Risotta a la Asgreen | 74
Salad Niçoise | 140
Salt'n'vinegar-potatoes | 200
Sheetpan ratatouille with chickpeas | 284
Stir-fry noodles with beef and veggies | 50
Thousand-layer potatoes | 240

BAKED AND SWEET STUFF A-Z

Baked cheese cake | 152
Oven baked nectarines with vanilla yoghurt and crumbl | 244
Banoffee dessert | 100
Burger buns | 224
Lemon cake with cheese frosting | 136
The yellow Tour cake | 188
Dulce de letche creme with baked plums | 76
Gluten free bread | 336
Gluten-free pancakes with fruit salad | 326
Dutch oven bread | 142
Potato power cake | 166
Raspberries with lemon curd and crispy filo | 280
Raspberry and orange cakes | 202
Polka-dot tiramisu | 226
Mads P's pancakes | 290
Pita bread | 90

Race cakes with cherries | 52
Tortilla pancakes | 212
Watt the fudge cake | 66
Apple strudel in filo | 254

CONDIMENTS A-Z

Dressings and sauces | 340
Stock and picke liquids | 342
Furikake sprinkles | 124
How to cut a chicken | 198
The Tour smoothie | 328

ENERGY BARS AND DRINKS A-Z

Baked banana bar | 312
Basic Raw bars | 312
Chocolate fudge | 312
Lemon cake with cheese frosting | 136
Potato power cake | 166
Race cakes with cherries | 52
Recovery protein drink | 313
Rice bars | 314
The Tour smoothie | 328
The yellow Tour cake | 188
Watt the fudge cake | 66

RECOMENDATIONS

Hydration powder: Adifferent.co

Books: *ROAR* and *NEXT LEVEL* by Dr. Stacy Sims
Eat Race Win by Hannah Grant
The Cake Cookbook by Hannah Grant

TV show: *Eat Race Win* on Amazon Prime

Podcast: *Hubermans Lab*

A huge thank you to my favorite ceramicists in Denmark.

Aage and Gitte Würtz ceramics
instagram: @wurtzaage
Web: aagewurtz.dk

MK ceramics
Magdalena and Michal Kałużny-Włodarek
instagram: @mkstudio_cph
Web: mk-ceramics.com

DISCLAIMER

Remember that everything in this book is indicative; it may be a good idea to consult a medical science or diet/nutrition professional if you decide to make major diet changes or have a health issue.

SOURCES

1. Omega-3 Fatty Acids for Sport Performance – Are They Equally Beneficial for Athletes and Amateurs? A Narrative Review Frank Thielecke[1,2,*] and Andrew Blannin[3] https://www.ncbi.nlm.nih.gov/pmc/articles/PMC7760705/

2. https://www.sciencedaily.com/releases/2022/10/221005162432.htm University of Texas Health Science Center at San Antonio. "Study links omega-3s to improved brain structure, cognition at midlife: Holy mackerel! Could eating salmon, cod, tuna, herring or sardines keep our brains healthy and our thinking agile in middle age?" ScienceDaily. ScienceDaily, 5 October 2022. <www.sciencedaily.com/releases/2022/10/221005162432.htm>.

3. https://www.ahajournals.org/doi/10.1161/JAHA.120.019814 Dietary Fatty Acids, Macronutrient Substitutions, Food Sources, and Incidence of Coronary Heart Disease: Findings From the EPIC-CVD Case-Cohort Study Across Nine European Countries Marinka Steur, Laura Johnson et. Al.

4. Jäger, R., Kerksick, C. M., Campbell, B. I., Cribb, P. J., Wells, S. D., Skwiat, T. M., … Antonio, J. (2017). International Society of Sports Nutrition Position Stand: protein and exercise. Journal of the International Society of Sports Nutrition, 14

5. Volpi E, Campbell WW, Dwyer JT, Johnson MA, Jensen GL, Morley JE, Wolfe RR. Is the optimal level of protein intake for older adults greater than the recommended dietary allowance? J Gerontol a Biol Sci Med Sci 2013;68:677–81

6. Volpi E, Campbell WW, Dwyer JT, Johnson MA, Jensen GL, Morley JE, Wolfe RR. Is the optimal level of protein intake for older adults greater than the recommended dietary allowance? J Gerontol a Biol Sci Med Sci 2013; 68:677–81

7. Low Calorie Dieting Increases Cortisol. A. Janet Tomiyama, Ph.D.,a Traci Mann et.al https://www.ncbi.nlm.nih.gov/pmc/articles/PMC2895000/

8. The Cake Cookbook, 2022 Hannah Grant

9. Low-carbohydrate, ketogenic diet impairs anaerobic exercise performance in exercise-trained women and men: a randomized-sequence crossover trial Kymberly A Wroble 1, Morgan N Trott et.al https://pubmed.ncbi.nlm.nih.gov/29619799/

10. Stacy Sims Ph.D. https://www.drstacysims.com/blog/Why-Women-Need-to-Prioritize-Protein

THANK YOU!

First of all, a big thank you to The Eagle. Bjarne "The Eagle" Riis was the man who gave me the job that has more or less defined my work life more than I could have ever imagined. Thanks to all the lovely riders and cycling legends who have participated. It has been so exciting to talk to you all.

A HUGE thank you to Ulrich Gorm Albrechtsen for helping me get in touch with many of the riders through the DCU.

I must be completely honest and say that this book is very special to me, and it has only been made possible through meeting with some amazingly passionate and sweet people that fate would have me meet, including my agent, Michael Benzon, my patient publisher, Jesper Helmin, and the super creative Johannes T. Hansen, who have been my kitchen helpers at the eleventh hour.

A huge thank you to all of you for believing in me and taking the chance to revive this legendary cookbook in a new format. I look forward to many more exciting projects with you guys.

Also, a huge thank you to my sweet boyfriend, Peter, for being completely unaffected and, yes, almost happy to live in the photo epicenter of the cookbook, where the lunch and dinner scheme has been invasive for a few weeks. Thank you very much for letting me be me with my work and crazy ideas.

Thanks to Ferdinand and the neighbors for eating the leftovers from photo sessions! I'm glad you liked them (otherwise, this would have been a big fat book of dishes that nobody likes).

Thank you to Erik, who has given me the confidence to rebrand myself and all the support I could dream of. Also, thanks to Mark for making such beautiful things for me.

Thanks to my sweet mother for being my mother and looking after my dog while this has been going on. I love you – just so you don't have any doubts.

Thanks to my many good old and new friends who have helped and supported me over the years, which has led up to today: Ilya, Sarah, Avalo, Christensen, Kristoffer, and the sweet Slow Boys, Henny and Michael. And, of course, also you, Anders. Thank you.

Last but not least, thanks to all the nice people who have supported me and bought my books over the years. This means so much to me.

Bon appétit!
HANNAH GRANT